New VEGETARIAN *food*

Christine McFadden

PHOTOGRAPHS BY MARIE-LOUISE AVERY

Collier Books
Macmillan Publishing Company
New York
Maxwell Macmillan International
NEW YORK OXFORD SINGAPORE SYDNEY

Collier Books
Macmillan Publishing Company
866 Third Avenue
New York, NY 10022

Macmillan Publishing Company is part of the
Maxwell Communication Group of Companies

Printed in Italy

Library of Congress Cataloging-in-Publication Data
McFadden, Christine
    New vegetarian food / Christine McFadden : photographs by Marie-Louise Avery.
        p.   cm.
    ISBN 0-02-034623-9
    1. Vegetarian cookery. 2. Cookery, Mediterranean. I. Title.
TX 837.M477   1994
641.5'636 – dc20   93-33435 CIP

Macmillan Books are available at special discounts for
bulk purchases for sales promotions, premiums, fund-raising, or
educational use. For details, contact:
Special Sales Director
Macmillan Publishing Company
866 Third Avenue New York NY 10022

First Collier Books Edition 1994

Managing Editor: ANNE MCDOWALL
Copy Editor: VERONICA SPERLING
Designer: PETER BRIDGEWATER
Photographer: MARIE-LOUISE AVERY
Home Economist: MEG JANSZ
Stylist: GLORIA NICOL
Typesetting: CHRIS LANAWAY
Illustrator: LORRAINE HARRISON
Indexer: ALISON LEACH
Colour reproduction:
P & W GRAPHICS PTE. LTD., SINGAPORE

CONTENTS

AUTHOR'S ACKNOWLEDGMENT

I would like to thank my husband, Ed, for his tireless washing up during the recipe testing. Many thanks also to Veronica Sperling, who edited this book, and to Alix Pirani, Anna Parry-Jones, Alex Roberts and Ulf and Wendy Martensson for their love and support throughout the project.

INTRODUCTION

Vegetarian cooking today is a very different affair from the brown rice and nut roasts of the 70s and early 80s. It is exciting and colorful, and focuses on taste and quality. In this book, my aim is to capture the vitality of new vegetarian cooking, and I hope it will inspire vegetarians and non-vegetarians alike to experiment and to share my passion for the wealth of vegetables, grains, herbs, spices and oils that are now available.

I have drawn on a diverse range of cuisines, from Eastern Europe to South America, but with an emphasis on Mediterranean-style cooking. The recipes combine the exotic with the traditional, but always make use of honest, fresh ingredients that naturally belong together and are not masked by too many interfering flavours.

The first chapter, *Vegetables*, provides perhaps the greatest source of inspiration. With their dazzling variety of color, texture, flavor and their tremendous versatility, vegetables are too good to be treated as a side dish. Here they are given the credit they deserve.

Grains, Beans, Peas and Nuts explores ingredients as old as civilization itself. Some may be unfamiliar to you, but all are delicious, and prepared with maximum emphasis on lightness and flavor.

Pasta, Pastry, Pancakes and Breads concentrates on time-honored staples – flour and water – which create a universal background to so many dishes.

The recipes in the appendix are mainly sauces, relishes and dressings – the elements that accent flavors and bring a dish to life with color and moistness. Although I have specified a sauce or dressing for each dish where appropriate, there are no hard and fast rules, so don't be afraid to mix and match.

Unfamiliar Ingredients

Some of the ingredients may be unfamiliar, and are not to be found in every supermarket. In most cases a substitute can be used, but it is worth trying to find the more obscure ingredients so that you can experience new flavors and expand your repertoire. One of my greatest pleasures is coming across unfamiliar ingredients in street markets, in foreign countries' supermarkets, ethnic stores and good health food stores. And there is now an increasing number of specialist mail order food companies, which supply unusual flours, grains, dried goods, spices and oils.

Herbs

I have used fresh herbs, but you can substitute 1 teaspoon of dried for 1 tablespoon of chopped fresh herbs. Most dried herbs benefit from dry-roasting to intensify the flavor. Place them in a small skillet without any oil. Heat gently, stirring, until they begin to give off their aroma.

Most supermarkets now sell a reasonable variety of fresh herbs, but there are many neglected varieties with magical flavors, such as lovage, hyssop and savory. These are worth growing yourself – even in a pot on a window-sill. I use a lot of cilantro, flat-leafed Italian parsley, arugula and sorrel, which are expensive to buy but easy to grow. Failing that, buy these herbs from ethnic stores where they are normally sold in large bunches.

Spices

As with dried herbs, spices benefit from dry-roasting to intensify their flavor. They lose their potency after a few months, so buy them in small quantities and store in airtight containers in a cool, dark place.

Pepper should always be freshly ground unless otherwise stated. For preference I use sea salt flakes. They have a different taste from ordinary sea salt, and provide beautiful little bursts of flavor on the tongue.

Lemons and Limes

Lemons and limes add an unmistakable but subtle sharpness to savory dishes. In most cases they can be interchanged, but limes do have a very special flavor. I have specified zest rather than peel, meaning the thin aromatic outer layer of the fruit rather than the rind. Use a special zesting tool or the fine grid on a grater.

Oils

It's worth investing in good quality extra virgin olive oil, particularly for salads. Groundnut oil is best for frying as it has a high smoke-point. Sunflower, grape-seed and safflower oils are good all-purpose oils that are not too heavy.

Go easy on toasted or dark sesame oil – it's more of a flavoring agent than a cooking oil. Flavor your salads with walnut, almond or hazelnut oil, especially if the salad contains nuts; or experiment with pistachio, pumpkin seed or pine nut oils – they add a beautiful depth of flavor to a dressing.

Seaweeds

Seaweeds are sometimes treated with suspicion, but these are one of the richest sources of minerals and vitamins needed by the body. Seaweeds are mostly imported from Japan, and are available dried in good health food stores. Used in moderation, they add a delicious flavor and texture to food. I have used the milder, sweet-flavored varieties such as arame, hiziki and nori.

Soy Sauce

I prefer to use the traditionally made Japanese soy sauces such as shoyu or tamari (wheat-free) as they have a comforting, warm, mellow flavor definitely not evident in other brands. You can buy shoyu and tamari in good health food stores.

Dried Beans and Peas

Garbanzo and other dried beans need soaking for 2 to 8 hours before cooking. The exact time depends on the age of the beans or peas as does the cooking time. I have usually specified the dry weight, but if you use pre-cooked or canned ones, double the quantity.

Some dried beans contain a toxin that can cause severe stomach upsets, and even death, if not destroyed by cooking. Always boil them rapidly for 15 minutes, then discard the cooking water, rinse, and cook.

Nuts

Although I have given quantities for the shelled weight, nuts should ideally be freshly cracked before use. Failing that, always buy shelled nuts in small quantities as they easily become rancid. Store in airtight containers in a cool place. The flavor of nuts becomes much richer if you dry-roast them first. Place a single layer in a roasting pan for 7 to 10 minutes at 350°F stirring occasionally, until they become golden, and impart a warm toasted aroma.

Other Notes

All spoon measures are level
Use fresh herbs in preference to dried
1 tablespoon chopped fresh herbs = 1 teaspoon dried
Always use fresh Parmesan cheese
All eggs are medium unless otherwise stated

VEGETABLES

*With their wealth of shapes, sizes and flamboyant colors, I find
vegetables one of the most irresistible ingredients available. Because we
eat different parts of the plant – buds, leaves, stems, flowers, roots
and tubers – vegetables provide an almost limitless variety of tastes,
textures and flavors.*

*Although the supermarkets offer an amazing variety of vegetables all the year
round, I am a great believer in seasonal produce. There is nothing to beat an early
winter parsnip, sweetened by the first frosts, or spring cabbages with crisp, squeaky leaves, or the
first tender fava beans.*

*Vegetables are one of the major sources of the essential health-promoting vitamins A, C and E, but from the
moment of harvest they begin to lose these valuable nutrients. Although there is nothing
to beat the sheer delight of freshly picked vegetables, you can still retain flavor and
nutrients if you buy your vegetables as you need them. Store them for the shortest
possible time in the salad drawer of the refrigerator or in a cool airy larder.
Do any chopping or slicing just before cooking, and avoid soaking
them. Heat also destroys nutrients, so I cook most vegetables as
briefly as possible to retain maximum flavor and goodness.*

CONTENTS

EGGPLANT AND MUSHROOM SATAY

SERVES 6

RICH AND FILLING, THIS DISH CAN BE SERVED ON ITS OWN
AS A STARTER, OR WITH RICE AS A MAIN COURSE.

18 crimini mushrooms, wiped	*Oil for brushing*
1 large eggplant (about 12	
ounces)	

MARINADE

6 tablespoons olive oil	*1 clove garlic, crushed*
3 tablespoons soy sauce	*Salt and pepper*
1 tablespoon wine vinegar	

TO SERVE

Shredded Cos lettuce	*Satay Sauce (page 108)*
Cucumber, cut into strips	

GARNISH

2 tablespoons finely chopped cilantro

❖ Cut the mushrooms in half. Cut the eggplant into ¾-inch slices, then cut each slice into 4 segments. Place the vegetables in a single layer in a non-metallic dish.

❖ Mix together the marinade ingredients, and spoon over the vegetables, making sure they are thoroughly coated. Let stand for at least 1 hour, turning occasionally.

❖ Thread pieces of mushroom and eggplant alternately onto 12 skewers. Brush with oil, and place under a pre-heated hot broiler or on a barbecue. Cook for 10 minutes, turning frequently and brushing with oil, until browned.

❖ Place on a bed of shredded lettuce and cucumber strips. Spoon over some of the satay sauce, and serve the remainder in a bowl. Sprinkle with the cilantro and serve immediately.

KOHLRABI CARPACCIO

SERVES 4

POPULAR IN CENTRAL AND EASTERN EUROPE, KOHLRABI IS A
MEMBER OF THE CABBAGE FAMILY BUT IT LOOKS LIKE A
TURNIP. IT CAN BE EATEN RAW OR COOKED. BUY IT WHEN
IT IS NO BIGGER THAN AN APPLE – LARGER SPECIMENS
TEND TO BE VERY HARD.

3 small kohlrabi, peeled	*3 tablespoons extra virgin*
(weighing about 3 ounces each)	*olive oil*
4 large radishes	*1 tablespoon walnut oil*
1 large carrot	*1 tablespoon snipped chives*
2 teaspoons orange juice	*¼ cup coarsely chopped*
2 teaspoons lime juice	*walnuts*
Salt and pepper	

❖ Using a mandoline or very sharp knife, slice the kohlrabi, radishes and carrot horizontally into paper-thin circles. Place in a shallow serving bowl.

❖ Whisk the citrus juices with the salt, pepper and oils. Pour the dressing over the vegetables, and toss well. Leave to stand for 1 hour at room temperature.

❖ Add the chives and walnuts just before serving.

EGGPLANT STIR-FRY WITH HOT SOUR SAUCE

EGGPLANTS BECOME SOFT AND SWEET WHEN STIR-FRIED – A PLEASING CONTRAST TO THE CRISP WATER CHESTNUTS AND THE SHARP SAUCE.

2 eggplants, peeled
2 red bell peppers, cored, seeded
and cut into matchstick
sized strips
6 tablespoons peanut oil
1 cup sliced water chestnuts
6 scallions, sliced diagonally
into ¾-inch lengths
1-inch piece fresh ginger root,
peeled and chopped very finely
2 cloves garlic, chopped
very finely

1 fresh green chili, deseeded
and chopped very finely
2 teaspoons sugar
1½ tablespoons soy sauce
⅔ cup Vegetable Stock
(page 111)
2 teaspoons cornstarch,
blended with a little water or
stock
1½ tablespoons rice vinegar
(or white wine vinegar)
1 teaspoon sesame seeds

GARNISH
Chopped scallion tops

❖ Slice the eggplants in half lengthwise. With the flat side facing downward, slice each half lengthwise into ¼-inch strips. Slice the wider strips lengthwise in half again, then cut all the strips crosswise into 1½-inch pieces.
❖ Heat 5 tablespoons of the oil in a wok or large skillet over a high heat until almost smoking. Add the eggplant and bell pepper strips, and stir-fry over a high heat for 2 to 3 minutes until just beginning to color. Remove from the pan, and drain on paper towels.
❖ Heat the remaining oil, and stir-fry the water chestnuts, scallions, ginger root, garlic and chili over a high heat for 1 minute.
❖ Return the eggplant and bell pepper to the wok or skillet, and add the sugar, soy sauce and stock. Stir-fry for 2 minutes over a medium heat.
❖ Add the cornstarch and cook for a minute, stirring, until thickened slightly. Stir in the vinegar and sesame seeds, and stir-fry for 30 seconds more.
❖ Garnish with scallion tops, and serve with boiled rice.

AVOCADO AND CHILI DIP

USE A GOOD VARIETY OF HERBS – ANY OR ALL OF THE FOLLOWING WOULD BE FINE: LOVAGE, ARUGULA, SORREL, SAVORY, THYME, PARSLEY, BASIL, CHIVES AND TARRAGON.

1 fat fresh green chili
2 medium-sized ripe avocados
1 tablespoon lime juice
Grated zest of 1 lime
3 tablespoons finely chopped
mixed herbs

⅓ cup ricotta cheese
1 clove garlic, crushed
2 teaspoons green
peppercorns, crushed
¼ teaspoon coarse sea salt
Herb sprigs, to garnish

❖ Place the chili under a hot broiler for 5 to 8 minutes, turning frequently, until the skin blisters and blackens. Remove the skin and seeds, and chop the flesh roughly.
❖ Peel the avocados, and chop the flesh roughly. Mix with the lime juice to prevent discoloration.
❖ Put the avocado in a food processor with the chili and remaining ingredients, and blend until smooth.
❖ Season to taste, adding more lime juice if necessary, and pour into a serving bowl. Garnish with sprigs of herbs.
❖ If not serving immediately, sprinkle with lime juice, cover tightly, and chill. Serve with pumpernickel or rye bread triangles.

GREEN BEAN AND ROASTED GARLIC SALAD

SERVES 6

IT IS WELL WORTH ROASTING THE GARLIC FOR THE
WONDERFULLY MELLOW FLAVOR. ROAST MORE CLOVES
THAN YOU NEED AND USE THEM TO FLAVOR OLIVE OILS
AND VINEGARS.

8 ounces fine green beans	*1 tablespoon balsamic vinegar*
6 ounces cherry tomatoes,	*1 tablespoon lime juice*
halved	*Salt and pepper*
1 tablespoon finely chopped	*1 tablespoon pine nuts*
basil	*3 large cloves garlic, unpeeled*
4 tablespoons extra virgin	*and left whole*
olive oil	*1 head of escarole*

❖ Steam the green beans over boiling water for 4 minutes until just tender but still crunchy. Refresh under cold water, drain, and pat dry with paper towels. Slice in half, and place in a bowl with the tomatoes and basil.

❖ Whisk 4 tablespoons of the olive oil with the vinegar, lime juice, salt and pepper. Pour over the green bean mixture.

❖ Put the pine nuts on a baking sheet and toast in the oven at 350°F for 2 minutes until golden brown.

❖ Increase the heat to 425°F and roast the garlic for 15 minutes. Remove the skins, chop roughly, and add to the green beans and tomatoes.

❖ Arrange the escarole leaves on a serving dish, and pile the green bean mixture on top. Scatter with pine nuts, and serve.

BAKED BELL PEPPERS WITH FETA

SERVES 4

SERVE THIS DISH WITH A CRISP GREEN SALAD AS A
LIGHT LUNCH OR EVENING MEAL.

1 each large red, green and	*1 cup fresh wholewheat bread*
yellow bell pepper	*crumbs*
Salt and pepper	*Grated zest of 1 lemon*
2 cloves garlic, chopped	*2 to 3 tablespoons olive oil*
very finely	*6 black olives, stoned and*
2 teaspoons each finely chopped	*sliced*
marjoram and parsley	*1 ounce feta cheese, cut into*
1 teaspoon finely chopped	*½-inch cubes*
rosemary	

❖ Place the bell peppers under a hot grill for 8 to 10 minutes, turning occasionally, until the skins begin to blacken. Cover or place in a sealed plastic bag for 5 minutes to loosen the skin. Remove the skin, core and seeds.

❖ Cut the flesh into bite-sized pieces, and place in a shallow ovenproof dish. Season with salt and pepper.

❖ Combine the garlic, herbs, bread crumbs and lemon zest. Season with pepper, and add the olive oil to bind the mixture together.

❖ Scatter the mixture over the peppers. Add the olives and feta cheese.

❖ Bake in the oven at 425°F for 10 to 15 minutes until crisp.

CARROT AND LOVAGE SOUP

SERVES 6

LOVAGE IS ONE OF THOSE OLD-FASHIONED HERBS WHICH COULD BE USED MORE OFTEN. IT HAS AN ASTRINGENT FLAVOR, SLIGHTLY REMINISCENT OF LIQUORICE. IF YOU CAN'T OBTAIN IT, USE BASIL OR CELERY LEAVES, OR A MIXTURE OF BOTH.

¼ cup/½ stick butter	4 tablespoons finely chopped
1 onion, chopped	lovage
1 pound carrots, sliced	5 cups Vegetable Stock (page 111)
8 ounces potatoes, sliced	Salt and pepper

GARNISH
6 tablespoons mild plain yogurt | Lovage leaves

❖ Melt the butter in a large pan. Add the onion, carrot, potato and lovage. Cover, and cook over a low heat for 10 minutes, stirring occasionally.

❖ Add the stock and season with salt and pepper. Bring to a boil, then simmer for 15 minutes.

❖ Liquidize the mixture until smooth. Reheat gently and check the seasoning.

❖ Serve each bowl with a swirl of yogurt and garnish with a lovage leaf.

MINTED SNOW PEA MOUSSE

SERVES 6

A DELICATELY FLAVORED FIRST COURSE FOR A SUMMER DINNER. SERVE IT WITH TRIANGLES OF RYE BREAD OR MELBA TOAST, AND CHILLED WHITE WINE.

10 ounces snow peas, trimmed	1 generous cup ricotta cheese
1¾ cups cold Vegetable Stock	½ cup heavy cream
(page 110)	4 heaped teaspoons
¼ teaspoon sugar	vegetarian gelatin
¼ teaspoon salt	4 tablespoons finely chopped
Pepper	mint
3 tablespoons mayonnaise	2 tablespoons lemon juice

GARNISH
6 mint sprigs

❖ Put the snow peas in a saucepan. Bring 6 tablespoons of the stock to a boil in another pan and pour over the snow peas. Cover, and simmer rapidly for 2 minutes, taking care that the liquid does not evaporate. The snow peas should still be crisp and bright green.

❖ In a blender or food processor, purée the snow peas with the cooking liquid, sugar, salt and pepper until smooth.

❖ Beat together the mayonnaise, ricotta and cream.

❖ Put the remaining cold stock in a saucepan. Sprinkle over the gelatin and stir until completely dissolved. Heat gently, stirring, until the mixture begins to steam. Do not allow to boil.

❖ Beat the dissolved gelatin into the ricotta mixture, then fold in the snow pea purée, mint and lemon juice. Add more salt and pepper if necessary.

❖ Pour into six ½-cup ramekin dishes, cover with plastic wrap, and chill. Garnish with a mint sprig before serving.

CELERIAC AND DILL SOUP

SERVES 4 TO 6

CELERIAC IS A SADLY NEGLECTED VEGETABLE
THAT DESERVES TO BE USED MORE WIDELY. WITH ITS
FRESH, NUTTY FLAVOR, IT MAKES A WELCOME ADDITION
TO WINTER SALADS.

¼ cup/½ stick butter or margarine
1 bay leaf
2 tablespoons chopped dillweed
1 onion, chopped finely
1 medium-sized celeriac (about
1¼ pounds), cut into small cubes

1 quart Strong Vegetable Stock
(page 111)
Salt and pepper
3 tablespoons light cream
2 teaspoons lemon juice

❖ Melt the butter or margarine in a saucepan with the bay leaf and half the dillweed. Simmer over a gentle heat for a minute or two to allow the flavors to develop.

❖ Add the onion and celeriac, cover, and simmer gently for about 10 minutes until they begin to soften.

❖ Add the stock and seasoning. Bring to a boil, cover and simmer for about 30 minutes until the vegetables are tender. Remove the bay leaf.

❖ Liquidize the mixture, then return to the pan and reheat. Remove from the heat, and stir in the cream, lemon juice and remaining dillweed. Check the seasoning, and serve.

GOLDEN GAZPACHO SOUP

SERVES 6

PREPARE THIS SUNSHINE-COLORED SOUP ONE DAY AHEAD.
YOU CAN USE RED TOMATOES BUT THE COLOR OF THE
SOUP WILL BE DIFFERENT.

2 x ½-inch thick slices white
bread, crusts removed, cubed
3 tablespoons olive oil
3 tablespoons white wine vinegar
Few drops of Tabasco sauce
3 large yellow bell peppers
1 small onion, unpeeled
2 large cloves garlic, unpeeled
½ cucumber, peeled, seeded and
chopped roughly

2 tender celery stalks, leaves
included, chopped roughly
1¼ pounds yellow cherry
tomatoes
3 cups cold Vegetable Stock
(page 111)
½ teaspoon sugar
1½ teaspoons lemon juice
Salt and pepper

TO SERVE

1 red bell pepper, cored, seeded
and diced finely
½ cucumber, peeled and
diced finely

9 scallions, chopped finely
Basil sprigs, to garnish

❖ Put the bread cubes on a baking sheet and bake at 350°F for about 10 minutes until pale golden. Let cool, then transfer to a large bowl. Increase the temperature to 400°F.

❖ Whisk together the oil, vinegar and Tabasco sauce. Pour over the bread, turning the cubes to coat. Let stand for 1 hour, turning occasionally.

❖ Place the yellow bell peppers and onion on a baking sheet, and roast for 20 minutes, turning occasionally. Add the garlic, and roast for 15 minutes until all the vegetables are tender.

❖ Let cool, then skin and deseed the bell peppers, and peel the onion and garlic. Transfer to a food processor with the bread cubes, and process to a chunky purée. Pour into a large bowl.

❖ Purée the cucumber, celery and tomatoes for 3 minutes. Push through a strainer, extracting as much moisture as possible. Add the strained vegetables to the bread mixture, mixing well. The mixture should be quite thick. Season to taste with salt and pepper. Cover, and chill overnight.

❖ Just before serving, add the sugar and lemon juice, and check the seasoning. Ladle into bowls, garnish with a sprig of basil, and serve with the diced vegetables.

STEAMED ROOTS WITH CHARBROILED TOMATO AND CHILI SAUCE

SERVES 4

A SATISFYING AND FILLING WINTER DISH. BE ADVENTUROUS WITH YOUR SELECTION OF ROOT VEGETABLES, AND INCLUDE SOME OF THE LESSER KNOWN VARIETIES – OR YOU CAN USE ONE SORT ONLY. YOU'LL NEED A TOTAL OF ABOUT 3 POUNDS.

½ celeriac	*1 eddo or colocassi (a Greek-*
2 potatoes	*Cypriot root vegetable)*
1 parsnip	*3 tablespoons butter*
2 kohlrabi	*2 tablespoons finely chopped*
½ sweet potato	*flat-leafed Italian parsley*
	Salt and pepper

SAUCE

2 pounds plum tomatoes	*½ onion, chopped very finely*
4 large cloves garlic, unpeeled	*½ teaspoon sugar*
2 fresh green chilies	*½ teaspoon salt*
2 teaspoons dried oregano	*Pepper*
or thyme	*1 tablespoon butter*
2 tablespoons olive oil	

❖ To make the sauce, place the tomatoes, garlic and chilies under a hot broiler. Turn frequently, until the skins blister and blacken. The chilies will need about 5 minutes, the garlic 10 to 15 minutes and the tomatoes 15 to 20 minutes.

❖ Peel the garlic, remove the skin and seeds from the chili, but do not peel the tomatoes.

❖ Dry-fry the oregano or thyme in a small heavy-based pan over a moderate heat for a few minutes until you can smell the aroma.

❖ Heat the oil in another small pan over a moderate heat. Gently fry the onion for about 5 minutes until translucent. Add the dry-fried oregano or thyme and fry for another minute.

❖ Purée the tomatoes, including any blackened bits of skin (they add to the flavor), with the garlic, chili and onion mixture until smooth.

❖ Pour into a large skillet and season with the sugar, salt and pepper. Simmer for 5 to 10 minutes, stirring occasionally, until some of the liquid has evaporated. Stir in the butter, and set aside.

❖ Meanwhile, peel the vegetables, and cut into even-sized ¼-inch thick slices. Place in a steamer set over a large pan of boiling water, putting the denser vegetables at the bottom. Cover tightly, and steam for 15 minutes or until just tender.

❖ Transfer the vegetables to a heated serving dish. Dot with the butter, and carefully stir in the parsley, salt and pepper.

❖ Reheat the sauce, and serve separately.

BAKED CUCUMBER IN DILLWEED AND MINT CREAM

`SERVES 4`

START THIS DISH AT LEAST THREE HOURS BEFORE YOU PLAN
TO SERVE IT, SO THAT THE CUCUMBERS HAVE TIME TO
DRAIN PROPERLY.

2 cucumbers	2 scallions, bulb and top,
1 tablespoon white wine	chopped finely
vinegar	Pepper
½ teaspoon salt	1 cup heavy cream
¼ teaspoon sugar	2 tablespoons each finely
2 tablespoons butter	chopped dillweed and mint
	¼ teaspoon paprika

GARNISH

Dillweed leaves	Paprika

❖ Peel the cucumbers, cut in 4 lengthwise and remove the seeds. Cut lengthwise into ¼-inch strips, then cut across into 2-inch pieces.

❖ Place in a large bowl, and toss with the vinegar, salt and sugar. Leave to stand for 2 hours. Drain, and pat dry on paper towels.

❖ Transfer the cucumber pieces to a shallow ovenproof dish. Melt the butter, and pour it over the cucumber. Stir in the scallions, and season with plenty of freshly ground black pepper. Bake at 350°F, stirring occasionally, for 45 minutes or until just tender.

❖ Meanwhile, bring the cream to a boil in a small saucepan. Stir in the dillweed, mint and paprika. Reduce the heat, and simmer for about 10 minutes until the cream has reduced. Season to taste with salt and pepper.

❖ Pour the cream over the cucumber, and garnish with dillweed leaves and a sprinkling of paprika.

CELERIAC, APPLE AND SORREL SALAD

`SERVES 4`

CELERIAC HAS A LOVELY FRESH, NUTTY TASTE WHICH GOES
WELL WITH THE LEMONY SHARPNESS OF SORREL. TO AVOID
BRUISING, TEAR THE SORREL LEAVES RATHER THAN
CUTTING WITH A KNIFE. IF SORREL IS UNAVAILABLE, USE
YOUNG SPINACH LEAVES OR ARUGULA INSTEAD.

2 small celeriac, weighing about	1½ cups young sorrel, stalks
1½ pounds total	removed and torn into shreds
Lemon juice	⅓ cup chopped walnuts
2 crisp red-skinned apples	

DRESSING

1 tablespoon lemon juice	Pepper
½ teaspoon sugar	3 tablespoons extra virgin
½ teaspoon Dijon mustard	olive oil
¼ teaspoon celery salt	1 tablespoon walnut oil

❖ Peel the celeriac and cut into ½-inch slices, sprinkling with lemon juice to prevent discoloration.

❖ Plunge into salted boiling water to which you have added 2 tablespoons of lemon juice. Bring back to a boil for 2 minutes.

❖ Drain under cold running water, and pat dry with paper towels.

❖ Cut the slices into ½-inch dice, and place in a salad bowl.

❖ Quarter and core the unpeeled apples, then cut into small dice, sprinkling with lemon juice as you work.

❖ Mix the apple with the celeriac, and add the sorrel and nuts.

❖ Whisk together the dressing ingredients. Pour over the salad just before serving, and toss gently.

ROASTED LEEKS AND CARROTS

SERVES 4

THE LEEKS SHOULD BE BROWN ON THE OUTSIDE AND TENDER INSIDE.

2 long carrots, cut lengthwise into eighths
8 small leeks, trimmed and left whole
1 small clove garlic, chopped finely

Pinch of dried herbes de Provence
¼ cup olive oil
Coarse sea salt
1 tablespoon finely chopped flat-leafed Italian parsley

❖ Pack the leeks and carrots closely together in a shallow ovenproof dish just large enough to hold them in a single layer. Scatter the garlic and herbes de Provence over the top. Add the olive oil, turning the vegetables to make sure they are well coated. Sprinkle with coarse sea salt.

❖ Place in the top of the oven at 500°F, and roast for 10 minutes. Turn and roast for another 10 minutes until the vegetables are beginning to blacken. Scatter with parsley and a little more sea salt to taste, and serve immediately.

ONION AND POTATO FRITTATA WITH SALSA VERDE

SERVES 4 TO 6

A FRITTATA IS AN ITALIAN OPEN OMELETE, COOKED UNTIL FIRM. SERVE HOT OR AT ROOM TEMPERATURE ACCOMPANIED BY A SALAD OF MIXED LEAVES AND PIQUANT GREEN SAUCE.

3 tablespoons olive oil
⅓ cup butter
2 onions, halved and thinly sliced
10 ounces cooked waxy potatoes, cut into ½-inch cubes
¼ cup shelled roughly chopped walnuts

Salt and pepper
8 eggs
⅓ cup freshly grated Parmesan
2 tablespoons finely chopped mixed herbs, e.g. thyme, basil, lovage and tarragon

TO SERVE
Salsa Verde (Piquant Green Sauce) (page 106)

❖ Heat 2 tablespoons of the olive oil and 2 tablespoons of the butter in a 10-inch non-stick skillet. Gently fry the onions over a medium-low heat for about 40 minutes until very soft, stirring frequently.

❖ Meanwhile, heat the remaining olive oil and 2 tablespoons of the butter in a pan. Gently fry the potatoes over a medium heat for about 2 minutes, then add the chopped walnuts. Continue to fry until the potatoes are golden on all sides – another 3 minutes or so.

❖ Combine the onions, potatoes and walnuts in a bowl. Season with salt and pepper, and allow to cool a little.

❖ Beat the eggs well, then stir in the Parmesan cheese, ¼ teaspoon salt, pepper, herbs and the onion mixture.

❖ Wipe out the pan in which you cooked the onions. Melt the remaining butter until foaming. Quickly pour in the egg mixture, stirring with a fork to spread out the filling.

❖ Cover, and cook over a low heat for 5 to 8 minutes until the eggs are almost set. Place briefly under a hot broiler until the surface is set but not brown. Slide onto a plate, cut into wedges, and serve with the sauce.

SAUTEED MUSHROOMS AND
JERUSALEM ARTICHOKES WITH SAGE

SERVES 4

USE A SELECTION OF WILD MUSHROOMS OR
CULTIVATED CRIMINI, LARGE FLAT CAP, SHIITAKE AND
OYSTER MUSHROOMS. BE CAREFUL NOT TO OVERCOOK THE
ARTICHOKES AS THEY TEND TO DISINTEGRATE.

12 ounces Jerusalem artichokes
¼ cup/½ stick butter
4 tablespoons olive oil
4 tablespoons finely chopped
sage
1¼ pounds mushrooms, cleaned
and cut into bite-sized pieces

2 cloves garlic, chopped finely
Salt and pepper
2 tablespoons lemon juice
1 tablespoon finely chopped
parsley
Triangles of fried bread, and
salad, to serve

❖ Peel the artichokes and cut into ½-inch chunks, placing in acidulated water to prevent browning.

❖ Heat half the butter and half the oil in a large skillet over a moderate heat. Add half the sage and fry for 30 seconds to flavor the oil. Add the artichokes and fry gently for 5 to 6 minutes until just beginning to color. Season with salt and pepper, and remove from the pan.

❖ Heat the remaining butter and olive oil, and fry the remaining sage for 30 seconds. Add the mushrooms, and stir-fry over a high heat for 7 to 10 minutes, or until most of the liquid has evaporated.

❖ Add the garlic, lemon juice and artichokes. Season generously, and stir-fry for another 1 to 2 minutes. Sprinkle with the parsley, and serve with fried bread and salad.

VEGETABLES ROASTED
WITH VINEGAR AND ROSEMARY

SERVES 4 TO 6

THIS SERVES 4 ON ITS OWN OR 6 AS AN ACCOMPANYING
DISH. IT IS DELICIOUS WITH ANY TYPE OF CASSEROLE.

8 small potatoes
4 small onions
2 small parsnips, cut into
2-inch lengths
2 large carrots, cut into
2-inch lengths
4 Jerusalem artichokes
1 small butternut squash,
peeled, seeded and cut into
1½-inch cubes
¼ cup/½ stick unsalted butter,
melted
2 tablespoons olive oil

3 tablespoons balsamic vinegar
2-3 sprigs rosemary
Sugar
1 teaspoon coriander seeds,
crushed
Coarse sea salt and coarsely
ground black pepper
2 tablespoons dry vermouth
¾ cup Strong Vegetable Stock
(page 111)
1 teaspoon cornstarch, blended
with a little water or stock
Flat-leafed Italian parsley, to
garnish

❖ Steam all the vegetables together over boiling water for 5 to 7 minutes until just becoming tender. Place in a roasting pan large enough to hold them in a single layer.

❖ Gently heat together the butter, olive oil, vinegar and rosemary, and pour over the vegetables. Sprinkle with a pinch of sugar and the coriander seeds, and season, turning the vegetables until well coated.

❖ Roast in the oven at 350°F, for about 1 hour, until evenly browned, basting and turning frequently. Transfer the vegetables to a heated serving dish.

❖ Place the roasting pan over a medium heat, and pour in the vermouth and stock. Bring to a boil, scraping up any sediment from the bottom of the pan. Simmer for a few minutes, then season with salt, pepper and a pinch more sugar. Add the cornstarch, and stir continuously until thickened. Strain and pour the sauce over the vegetables, and garnish with parsley.

BROCCOLI AND WATER CHESTNUT SALAD

SERVES 4

MARINATING THIS DISH WILL ALLOW THE FLAVORS TO
DEVELOP. HOWEVER, IF YOU'RE IN A RUSH IT'S JUST AS
DELICIOUS WHILE STILL WARM.

12 ounces broccoli florets
4 ounces water chestnuts, halved
1 tablespoon rice vinegar (or white wine vinegar)
2 tablespoons tamari (Japanese soy sauce)

3 tablespoons extra virgin olive oil
½-inch piece fresh ginger root, peeled and crushed in a garlic press
1½ teaspoons sesame seeds, toasted

❖ Steam the broccoli florets over boiling water for 3 to 5 minutes until bright green and still crisp. Put in a bowl with the water chestnuts.
❖ Whisk together the remaining ingredients, season, and pour over the broccoli, turning well to coat.
❖ Cover, and let marinate at room temperature for at least 1 hour before serving.

ARUGULA AND BROILED BELL PEPPER SALAD WITH PARMESAN CHEESE

SERVES 4

THE PEPPERY FLAVOR OF THE ARUGULA BALANCES THE
SWEETNESS OF THE BELL PEPPER.

1 red bell pepper
1 clove garlic, diced finely
2 teaspoons balsamic vinegar
Salt and pepper

5 tablespoons extra virgin olive oil
1½ ounce piece fresh Parmesan
1½ cups trimmed arugula

❖ Place the bell pepper under a hot broiler for about 15 minutes, turning occasionally, until blackened on all sides. Remove the skin, core and seeds, then slice into matchstick strips.
❖ Combine the garlic, vinegar, salt and pepper, then whisk in the olive oil. Using a swivel peeler, shave the Parmesan cheese into wafers.
❖ Place the arugula on four plates, and arrange the bell pepper strips on top. Pour a little dressing over the leaves. Sprinkle with the Parmesan shavings, and serve at once.

RAGOUT OF YOUNG VEGETABLES

SERVES 6

½ cup/½ stick butter	6 ounces sugar snap peas, or
6 pearl onions, halved	snow peas
lengthwise	1 pound young fava beans,
2 to 3 sprigs of thyme	shelled and outer skin removed
8 baby zucchini	2 tablespoons finely chopped
15 baby carrots	mixed herbs
8 baby corn ears	Juice of 1 lemon
8 ounces thin asparagus, cut	1 clove garlic, chopped finely
into 2-inch lengths	Salt and pepper

❖ Bring a large saucepan of salted water to a boil.

❖ Melt 2 tablespoons of the butter in a large skillet. Add the onions, thyme, ¾ cup of water and a pinch of salt. Bring to a boil, cover and simmer for 5 minutes.

❖ Meanwhile, blanch the vegetables separately in the order listed, allowing 2 minutes each for the squash and carrots and 1 minute each for the other vegetables. Make sure the water comes back to a boil before adding each one.

❖ As each batch of vegetables is blanched, remove with a slotted spoon, and add to the onions. Stir, cover, and continue to simmer. Add a little more water if the mixture becomes dry.

❖ When all the vegetables are in the pan, stir in the herbs, lemon juice, garlic and remaining butter. Season to taste. Stir over a high heat until the butter melts and the sauce thickens slightly.

FENNEL AND CARROT SALAD

SERVES 4

2 fennel bulbs	2 tablespoons orange juice,
3 carrots	strained
2 tablespoons pine nuts, toasted	6 tablespoons extra virgin olive
1 tablespoon white wine	oil
vinegar	Salt and pepper
	2 to 3 heads romaine lettuce

GARNISH
Snipped fennel leaves

❖ Cut off the base and top of the fennel, reserving the feathery green leaves. Remove the tough outer layers, then cut each bulb lengthwise into four. Cut away the woody center, then slice the segments lengthwise into narrow strips. Place in a bowl.

❖ Peel the carrots, and cut in half crosswise. Using a swivel peeler, shave away wide ribbons of carrot, working from opposite sides. Mix the carrot ribbons with the fennel, and add the toasted pine nuts.

❖ Whisk together the vinegar, orange juice, oil and seasoning. Pour over the carrot mixture, tossing well to coat.

❖ Arrange the lettuce leaves around the edge of a shallow serving dish. Pile the carrot mixture on top, and garnish with snipped fennel leaves.

ROASTED CHILI ROULADE

SERVES 6

AN IMPRESSIVE MAIN COURSE AND NOT AS DIFFICULT AS IT
LOOKS. JUST BE BRAVE WHEN INVERTING THE ROULADE!
THE DISH IS NOT OVERWHELMINGLY FIERY –
ROASTING THE CHILIES MELLOWS THE FLAVOR AND
THE EGGS CALM DOWN THE HEAT.

1½ cups milk	*⅓ cup butter*
½ teaspoon cumin seeds, toasted	*5 tablespoons all-purpose flour*
1 teaspoon coriander seeds, toasted	*½ teaspoon salt*
	5 eggs, separated
6 peppercorns	*4 tablespoons finely chopped cilantro*
4 fat fresh red chilies	
4 large cloves garlic, unpeeled	*3 tablespoons freshly grated Parmesan*

FILLING

1 scant cup ricotta cheese	*1 small avocado*
1 to 2 tablespoons milk	*1 tablespoon lime juice*
Grated zest of 1 lime	*10 cherry tomatoes, cut in 6*
Salt and pepper	*1 tablespoon finely chopped cilantro*

GARNISH
Cherry tomato slices

TO SERVE
Mixed leaf salad

❖ Grease and line a 12-inch square shallow baking pan with well-oiled baking parchment. Sprinkle with flour, tapping off any excess.

❖ Heat the milk in a small saucepan over a low heat with the cumin seeds, coriander seeds and peppercorns. Let infuse for 30 minutes. Pour the milk through a strainer to remove the seeds.

❖ Roast the chilies and garlic in the oven at 425°F, for 20 minutes, turning occasionally, until the skins begin to blister and blacken. Remove the skin and seeds from the chilies, and the skin from the garlic. Chop the flesh roughly.

❖ Melt the butter in a saucepan, add the flour and cook, stirring constantly, for 2 minutes. Whisk in the hot strained milk, and cook for 3 to 4 minutes, stirring constantly. Season with the salt, and let cool a little.

❖ Put the roasted chilies and garlic in a blender with a little of the white sauce, and purée until smooth. Stir the mixture into the sauce in the pan.

❖ Beat the egg yolks in a large mixing bowl. Beat in a little of the sauce, then gradually beat in the rest. Fold in the chopped cilantro and Parmesan cheese.

❖ Stiffly beat the egg whites with a pinch of salt. Using a metal spoon, carefully fold in 1 tablespoon of egg white to loosen the chili mixture, then fold in the remainder.

❖ Pour the mixture into the prepared pan, spreading it into the corners and leveling the surface. Bake in the oven at 400°F for 15 minutes until brown and puffed.

❖ Allow to settle for a few minutes, then turn out on to a clean dish cloth. Leave for 5 minutes, then carefully remove the baking parchment. Trim the edges neatly.

❖ Mix the ricotta with just enough milk to make a spreading consistency. Stir in the lime zest, and season to taste. Spread the over the base, leaving a small border all round.

❖ Peel and finely dice the avocado and mix with the lime juice, tomato and cilantro. Scatter the mixture over the ricotta, and season with salt and pepper.

❖ Carefully roll up like a jelly roll and transfer to a serving dish, seam-side down. Garnish with tomato, and serve with a mixed leaf salad.

VEGETABLE KEBABS WITH CILANTRO SAUCE

SERVES 4

2 corn-on-the-cob, sliced into
¾-inch rounds
8 firm cherry tomatoes
2 red onions, cut into 3-layer
1-inch pieces
1 red and 1 yellow bell pepper,
seeded and cut into
1-inch pieces
2 small zucchini, cut into
½-inch chunks
16 small shiitake mushrooms,
stems removed

⅓ cup butter
3 tablespoons olive oil
1 clove garlic, chopped
very finely
½ teaspoon cumin seeds,
crushed
1 teaspoon coriander seeds,
crushed
Pinch of cayenne pepper
Salt and pepper
Cilantro Sauce (page 107), to
serve

❖ Prepare the vegetables and thread onto 8 skewers.
❖ Melt the butter with the olive oil, garlic, spices and seasonings.
❖ Brush the kebabs with the melted butter mixture. Place under a hot broiler or over a barbecue. Cook for 15 minutes, turning and basting frequently, until just tender and beginning to blacken around the edges.
❖ Serve with the cilantro sauce.

BROILED EGGPLANT SALAD

SERVES 4

THE EGGPLANTS BROWN VERY QUICKLY
UNDER THE BROILER. TAKE CARE NOT TO BURN THEM.

2 small eggplants
1 red onion
⅔ cup olive oil
¼ teaspoon dried red pepper
flakes
½ teaspoon cumin seeds

½ teaspoon sesame seeds
2 cloves garlic, chopped very
finely
¼ teaspoon salt
Pepper
2 tablespoons lime juice

DRESSING

⅔ cup yogurt, strained
through a cheesecloth
2 tablespoons finely chopped
cilantro

Grated zest of ½ lime
1 clove garlic, chopped very
finely
Salt and pepper

GARNISH

Slices of lime | Cilantro leaves

❖ Cut the eggplants into ½-inch slices, and the onion into ¼-inch slices. Keep the onion rings in one piece by inserting two toothpicks from the outer ring to the center. Put the eggplant and onion in a large bowl.
❖ Combine the olive oil, red pepper flakes, cumin and sesame seeds, garlic, salt and pepper. Pour the mixture over the eggplant and onion slices, turning to coat. Marinate for at least 30 minutes.
❖ Meanwhile, mix together the yogurt, cilantro, lime zest, garlic, salt and pepper. Let stand at room temperature.
❖ Cook the vegetables on a rack under a hot broiler for about 5 minutes on each side, until slightly blackened. Allow to cool.
❖ Remove the toothpicks from the onion slices, and cut each slice in four. Cut the smaller eggplant slices in half, and the larger ones in four.
❖ Mix the onion and eggplant in a serving bowl, and sprinkle with the lime juice. Carefully fold in the yogurt mixture. Let stand at room temperature for about 1 hour.
❖ Garnish with lime slices and cilantro leaves. Serve with warm naan bread.

⊠ 🌾 ⊠ 🪶 ⊠

ORIENTAL-STYLE RATATOUILLE

SERVES 6

THE VEGETABLES ARE LIGHTLY COOKED TO RETAIN THEIR
SHAPE AND COLOR. THE DISH MAY BE SERVED HOT OR COLD
AS A STARTER, OR SERVED HOT AS A MAIN COURSE
ACCOMPANIED BY A GRAIN DISH AND A GREEN SALAD.

6 tablespoons olive oil
1 small onion, chopped finely
2 cloves garlic, chopped finely
2 cups peeled and chopped ripe
*   plum tomatoes*
2 tablespoons tamari (Japanese
*   soy sauce)*
5 teaspoons rice wine (or dry
*   sherry)*
1 teaspoon sugar
Salt and pepper
1 fresh green chili, seeded and
*   chopped finely*

2 teaspoons coriander seeds,
toasted and crushed
1 small eggplant, cut into
¾-inch chunks
1½ cups thickly sliced shiitake
mushrooms
2 small zucchini, cut into
½-inch diagonal slices
1 yellow and 1 red bell pepper,
cored, seeded and sliced
2 teaspoons sesame seeds,
toasted

❖ Heat 2 tablespoons of the oil in a saucepan. Gently fry the onion for 5 minutes until soft. Add the garlic, and fry for 30 seconds. Stir in the tomatoes, tamari, rice wine or sherry and sugar. Season with salt and pepper to taste.

❖ Simmer over a low heat, stirring occasionally, while the vegetables are cooking. The sauce should reduce and thicken slightly.

❖ Heat the remaining oil in a large pan, and stir-fry the chili and coriander seeds for a minute or two.

❖ Add the eggplants and mushrooms, and stir-fry over a medium heat for 5 minutes.

❖ Add the remaining vegetables, with more oil if necessary, and stir-fry for 5 minutes.

❖ Stir in the tomato sauce. Cover, and simmer for 10 minutes. Season to taste, and stir in the sesame seeds.

ARUGULA AND PARSLEY SOUP

SERVES 6

USE FLAT-LEAFED ITALIAN PARSLEY AS IT HAS A BETTER
FLAVOR. IF YOU CAN'T OBTAIN ARUGULA, MAKE THE SOUP
WITH PARSLEY INSTEAD.

3 cups flat-leafed Italian parsley
¼ cup/½ stick butter
1 medium-sized potato, sliced
2½ cups sliced leeks
2 cups sliced celery

1½ quarts Vegetable Stock
(page 111)
3 cups arugula
¾ cup light cream
Salt and pepper

TO SERVE
Fried bread croûtons

❖ Remove the stalks from the parsley, and chop them roughly.

❖ Melt the butter in a large saucepan. Add the chopped parsley stalks, potato, leeks and celery. Cover the pan, and cook over a low heat for about 10 minutes, stirring occasionally. Add the stock, bring to a boil, and simmer for 15 minutes.

❖ Roughly chop a handful of parsley and arugula leaves, and set aside. Add the remaining leaves to the pan, bring to a boil and simmer for a minute or two. The leaves should remain bright green.

❖ Liquidize the mixture, then pass through a strainer, and return to the pan. Season to taste. Add the cream, and reheat gently. Check the seasoning.

❖ Garnish each bowl with the reserved chopped leaves, and serve with croûtons.

PRESSED SPINACH AND GOAT CHEESE TERRINE WITH NORI

SERVES 8

A COLORFUL AND REFRESHING DISH FOR A SUMMER DINNER.
START IT THE DAY BEFORE YOU PLAN TO SERVE IT AND BE
PREPARED TO SPEND AN HOUR OR SO ON THE PREPARATION.
NORI IS A DELICATELY FLAVORED JAPANESE SEA
VEGETABLE NORMALLY USED FOR MAKING SUSHI ROLLS.
SOME BRANDS ARE ALREADY PRE-TOASTED, OTHERWISE
WAVE THE SHEETS OVER A GAS FLAME OR PLACE UNDER A
HOT GRILL FOR A FEW SECONDS.

16 to 18 spinach leaves, stems removed, or 5 ounces trimmed bok choy leaves
2 large yellow bell peppers
. 1 fennel bulb, trimmed, quartered and separated into layers

12 plum tomatoes with a good flavor
2 x 8-inch squares toasted nori
Pepper
2 tablespoons each finely chopped parsley and chives
6-8 torn basil leaves
2 cups crumbled dry goat cheese

TO SERVE
Mixed leaves, e.g. chicory, butterhead, lamb's lettuce, radicchio
Extra virgin olive oil

❖ Plunge the spinach leaves into boiling water for 30 seconds. Drain, and cool completely under cold water. Spread out on paper towels to dry.

❖ Place the peppers under a hot broiler for 10 minutes, turning occasionally, until the skins begin to blacken and blister. Place in a sealed plastic bag for 5 minutes, then remove the skin, core and seeds. Cut the flesh into matchstick-sized strips.

❖ Plunge the fennel pieces into boiling water for 4 minutes. Drain under cold running water, then dry with paper towels, and chop finely.

❖ Put the tomatoes in a bowl, pour over boiling water, and leave for 1 minute. Drain, and remove the skins. Cut into ¼-inch slices, discard the seeds, chop roughly, and drain.

❖ Line a 8-inch square cake pan with greased foil. Place a sheet of nori in the bottom of the pan. Cover with a layer of spinach or bok choy leaves, overlapping them neatly so there are no gaps. Season with pepper and a sprinkling of the herbs.

❖ Crumble half the goat cheese over the spinach, followed by half the tomatoes. Season with pepper and add more herbs.

❖ Add the bell peppers and fennel, spreading out the pieces evenly. Season again with pepper and herbs.

❖ Add the remaining tomatoes and goat cheese and season with pepper and herbs. Gently flatten the mixture, pushing it into the corners and sides of the pan. Top with the remaining spinach leaves.

❖ Place the second sheet of nori on top, pressing it down gently with the palm of your hand. Cover with a double thickness of greased foil. Press down with a heavy weight and chill in the refrigerator for at least 8 hours.

❖ Invert the pan over a cutting board and remove the foil. Cut the terrine into 4 squares, using an electric carving knife if possible. Carefully cut each square in half diagonally.

❖ Arrange a few lettuce leaves on eight plates, and sprinkle with olive oil. Place triangles of terrine on top.

BEETS ROASTED WITH CHILI, GARLIC AND THYME

SERVES 4

A DISH TO CONVERT EVEN THE MOST HARDENED BEET HATER. USE RAW BEETS RATHER THAN PRE-COOKED AS THEY HAVE A MUCH SUBTLER FLAVOR. THE SLIGHT SWEETNESS IS OFFSET BY THE CHILI AND GARLIC.

4 tablespoons olive oil
1 pound raw beets, peeled and quartered
Salt and pepper
1 tablespoon finely chopped thyme, or 1½ teaspoons dried herbes de Provence

1-2 fresh red chilies, seeded and chopped roughly
4 large cloves garlic, unpeeled
Finely chopped thyme, to garnish

❖ Put the oil in a small roasting pan and place in the oven at 400°F for 5 minutes until very hot.
❖ Add the beets, turning well to coat. Season generously with salt and pepper, and add the thyme.
❖ Roast for 45 minutes, turning occasionally, then add the chili and garlic. Roast for another 40 minutes until the garlic is very soft and purée-like.
❖ Remove the garlic skin, and stir the purée into the oil. Transfer to a warm serving dish, and pour the oil from the pan over the beets. Garnish with fresh thyme.
❖ Serve with a green salad and boiled polenta, using the polenta to mop up the delicious garlicky oil.

TRI-COLOR CABBAGE WITH CILANTRO AND SESAME

SERVES 4

IF YOU DON'T HAVE A STEAMER, COOK THE CABBAGE IN VERY LITTLE WATER, KEEPING THE RED CABBAGE SEPARATE.

¼ each of red, white and savoy cabbages
2 teaspoons sesame seeds
3 tablespoons butter

Coarse sea salt
Pepper
3 tablespoons finely chopped cilantro leaves

❖ Cut the cabbages in wedges, and slice away the core. Cut crosswise into fine slices, discarding any thick ribs.
❖ Place the red cabbage in the bottom of a large steamer basket with the savoy and white cabbage on top. Cover, and steam over boiling water for 5 minutes. The cabbage should be tender but still crunchy and the colors bright.
❖ Meanwhile, dry-fry the sesame seeds over a moderate heat until the aroma is released. Melt the butter in a small saucepan. Add the sesame seeds.
❖ Making sure any liquid from the red cabbage has dripped from the base of the steamer basket, transfer the cabbage to a heated serving dish. Season generously with sea salt and pepper. Pour the melted butter over the cabbage, sprinkle with the cilantro, and toss gently to mix the colors.

TOMATO AND BREAD SOUP

SERVES 4·6

A MEAL IN ITSELF, THIS VERY THICK TUSCAN-STYLE TOMATO SOUP NEEDS ONLY A GREEN SALAD TO ACCOMPANY IT. SERVE WITH PLENTY OF EXTRA BREAD TO DUNK IN THE SOUP.

7 tablespoons olive oil	*Salt and pepper*
1 tablespoon finely chopped sage	*4 large cloves garlic, sliced very thinly*
8 tablespoons finely chopped basil	*2½ tablespoons tomato paste*
2 onions, chopped finely	*3 pounds canned chopped tomatoes*
1¼ cups finely diced celery, leaves included	*3 cups Vegetable Stock (page 111)*
2 cups thinly sliced savoy cabbage	*6 ounces day-old Italian bread, cut into 1-inch cubes*

TO SERVE
Coarsely grated Parmesan

❖ Heat 3 tablespoons of the oil in a large, heavy-based saucepan over a moderate heat. Add the sage and half the basil and gently fry for 1 minute to flavor the oil.

❖ Add the onions and gently fry for about 7 minutes until soft. Add the celery, cabbage, garlic and salt and pepper. Gently fry for another 5 minutes.

❖ Stir in the tomato paste, tomatoes and stock. Bring to a boil, then cover, and simmer gently for 1½ to 2 hours, topping up with stock or water if necessary.

❖ Place the bread cubes on a baking sheet, and toast in the oven at 300°F for 5 minutes.

❖ Place the bread in a large saucepan. Pour the remaining olive oil over the bread, and allow it to soak in.

❖ Pour the soup over the bread, and let stand for 15 minutes. Reheat gently, stir in the remaining basil, and check the seasoning.

❖ Make sure each serving includes some of the bread from the bottom of the pan. Serve with grated Parmesan.

ENDIVE AND TOMATO GRATIN

SERVES 4

CHOOSE A DISH JUST BIG ENOUGH TO HOLD THE ENDIVE WITHOUT LEAVING GAPS IN BETWEEN.

4 large plump heads of endive, halved lengthwise	*2 teaspoons finely chopped marjoram or oregano*
Salt and pepper	*⅓ cup dry bread crumbs*
Olive oil	*⅓ cup freshly grated Parmesan*
2 cloves garlic, chopped finely	*¼ cup/½ stick butter*
1 x 7-ounce can chopped tomatoes	

❖ Make two or three deep cuts in the base of the endive heads. With the cut-side down, place under a hot broiler for 3 to 5 minutes until just beginning to blacken. Turn over, sprinkle with salt and pepper, and brush generously with olive oil, working the oil between the leaves. Cook, cut-side upward, for 10 to 15 minutes until just tender. Transfer the endive to a shallow ovenproof dish.

❖ Meanwhile, heat 1 tablespoon of olive oil in a small saucepan. Add the garlic and gently fry over a low heat for 30 seconds, then add the tomatoes and marjoram. Season to taste with salt and pepper. Simmer for 5 minutes, stirring occasionally, then pour the mixture over the chicory.

❖ Combine the bread crumbs and Parmesan cheese, and sprinkle over the endive. Dot with the butter, and bake at 375°F for 10 minutes or until crisp.

ARUGULA AND PINE NUT SOUFFLE

SERVES 4

ARUGULA IS WORTH GROWING YOURSELF AS IT IS EXPENSIVE TO BUY AND AVAILABLE ONLY IN SMALL PACKETS.

3½ cups trimmed arugula
¼ cup pine nuts
⅓ cup butter
2 tablespoons all-purpose flour
¾ cup milk

4 tablespoons freshly grated Parmesan
Salt and pepper
4 egg yolks
5 egg whites
⅛ teaspoon cream of tartar

TO SERVE
Cherry tomato salad

❖ Steam the arugula for 5 minutes until just wilted. Purée in a blender until smooth. Reheat with 2 tablespoons of the butter.

❖ Toast the pine nuts in the oven at 400°F for 2 minutes, until golden-brown. Chop roughly, and set aside.

❖ Place a metal baking sheet in the oven, and maintain the temperature.

❖ Melt the remaining butter in a saucepan. Add the flour, and stir to a smooth paste. Gradually add the milk, stirring constantly over a medium heat until it comes to a boil.

❖ Remove from the heat, and stir in the puréed arugula, the pine nuts and half the grated Parmesan. Season generously with salt and pepper.

❖ Transfer the mixture to a large bowl, then whisk in the egg yolks one at a time.

❖ Beat the egg whites with the cream of tartar until stiff. Fold 1 tablespoon of egg white into the arugula mixture to loosen it. Then carefully fold in the remainder, using a metal spoon.

❖ Grease a 2-quart soufflé dish, and sprinkle it with the remaining Parmesan, tipping out the surplus. Pour in the soufflé mixture, and scatter over any surplus cheese.

❖ Carefully place the dish on the baking sheet in the oven, and close the oven door gently. Immediately reduce the temperature to 375°F. Bake for 30 minutes, and serve immediately.

WATERCRESS CUSTARDS WITH CARROT AND ORANGE SAUCE

SERVES 6

A VERY PRETTY FIRST
COURSE WITH CITRUSY UNDERTONES.

*3 large bunches watercress,
stalks removed and chopped
roughly*
*¾ cup Vegetable Stock (page
111)*

2 large eggs
2 large egg yolks
1¼ cups heavy cream
Grated zest of 1 lemon
Salt and pepper

SAUCE

*5 ounces baby carrots, cut
into very thin diagonal slices*
*6 tablespoons Vegetable Stock
(page 111)*
2 tablespoons orange juice
¼ cup butter

*½ teaspoon finely chopped
rosemary*
Pinch of sugar
Salt and pepper
1 tablespoon heavy cream

GARNISH
6 watercress sprigs

❖ Generously butter six ½ cup oval ramekin dishes, and place a piece of buttered baking parchment in the bottom of each.

❖ Put the watercress in a saucepan. Bring the stock to a boil in another pan. Pour it over the watercress. Cover, and cook rapidly for about 1 minute until the watercress just wilts.

❖ Purée the watercress in a food processor with the cooking liquid, and let cool a little.

❖ Beat the eggs and yolks, then gradually beat in the watercress purée. Stir in the cream, lemon zest and seasoning.

❖ Pour the mixture into the prepared ramekin dishes. Place in a deep roasting pan with enough hot water to come halfway up their sides, and bake in the oven at 350°F, for 30 to 35 minutes until set.

❖ To make the sauce, put the carrots, stock and orange juice in a small saucepan with 1 tablespoon of the butter, the rosemary, sugar, salt and pepper. Bring to a boil, then simmer gently, uncovered, for 3 to 4 minutes. The carrots should be only lightly cooked.

❖ Dice the remaining butter, and add to the pan with the cream. Stir over a medium heat until the butter has melted. Raise the heat, and simmer rapidly for 2 minutes until the sauce has reduced and thickened slightly. Remove from the heat, and set aside.

❖ Remove the ramekin dishes from the oven, and leave to rest for a few minutes. Turn out onto six warmed plates.

❖ Garnish with a watercress sprig, and one or two slices of carrot from the sauce. Pour a little of the remaining sauce onto each plate, and serve at once.

GREEN BEAN AND KOHLRABI
SALAD WITH LEMON GRASS AND MINT

SERVES 4

A TRADITIONAL THAI FLAVORING, LEMON GRASS HAS A SUBTLE, WARM, LEMONY-LIME FLAVOR. YOU CAN USE GRATED LEMON ZEST INSTEAD BUT IT IS NOT AS GOOD.

8 ounces fine green beans, trimmed and cut into 2-inch pieces
1 kohlrabi, weighing about 4 ounces
½ cup/¼-inch diced yellow bell pepper
2 large lemon grass stalks
½ cup Vegetable Stock (page 111)

1 small clove garlic, chopped finely
½ teaspoon coriander seeds, toasted and crushed
3 tablespoons olive oil
Salt and pepper
2 teaspoons finely chopped mint
½ fresh red chili, seeded and sliced very finely, to garnish

❖ Place the beans in a steamer over boiling water, and steam for 3 to 4 minutes until tender but still crunchy. Drain under cold running water, and dry with paper towels.
❖ Peel the kohlrabi, and slice thinly. Stack a few slices together at a time and cut into matchstick-sized strips.
❖ Put the beans, kohlrabi and bell pepper in a bowl.
❖ Remove and discard the tough, outer leaves of the lemon grass. Cut the center crosswise into very thin slices. Place in a saucepan with the stock, and simmer for 10 minutes.
❖ Pour the lemon grass and stock into a blender with the garlic, coriander, olive oil, and seasoning. Purée until smooth.
❖ Pour the dressing over the vegetables. Add the mint, and toss gently. Garnish with finely sliced chili. Let stand.

MUSHROOM AND YELLOW BELL PEPPER SALAD

SERVES 4 TO 6

TRIM THE STALKS FROM THE SHIITAKE MUSHROOMS AS THEY CAN BE QUITE TOUGH. USE A VERY LARGE PAN, OR FRY THE MUSHROOMS IN BATCHES IF NECESSARY.

2 yellow bell peppers
4 tablespoons olive oil
6 tablespoons walnut oil
1 tablespoon balsamic vinegar
4 tablespoons chopped lovage or basil
Salt and pepper

12 ounces each oyster and shiitake mushrooms, cut into segments if large
2 cloves garlic, chopped finely
½ cup roughly chopped walnuts
1 head radicchio
Handful each of lamb's lettuce and arugula

❖ Place the yellow bell peppers under a hot broiler for about 15 minutes, turning occasionally, until blackened on all sides. Remove the skin, core and seeds. Cut the flesh into strips about 1½ inch long, and place in a shallow dish.
❖ Whisk together the olive oil, 2 tablespoons of the walnut oil, all the vinegar, 3 tablespoons of the lovage, and seasoning. Pour over the bell pepper strips.
❖ Heat 3 tablespoons of the walnut oil in a large skillet over a high heat until it begins to smoke. Add the mushrooms, and stir-fry for 10 minutes. Add the garlic, and stir-fry for another minute. Add to the peppers in the dish, turning well to coat. Let stand for at least 1 hour.
❖ Heat the remaining walnut oil, add the walnuts, and stir-fry for 1 minute. Remove from the pan, and set aside.
❖ Place the salad leaves in a bowl, and toss with half the mushroom mixture and half the walnuts. Pile the remaining mushroom mixture on top, and garnish with the remaining lovage and walnuts.

GRAINS, BEANS, PEAS AND NUTS

Thousands of years ago, grains and pulses changed the nature of civilization. Being the first foods that could be stored, they enabled our nomadic ancestors to establish settled communities, and to survive for long periods. It is not surprising, therefore, that grains and pulses have a quality unequalled by any other food. There is hardly a country in the world that does not have a grain or bean-based dish as part of its traditional cuisine – the rich cassoulets of France, Caribbean rice and peas, Indian dhal, Mexican refried beans.

The ingredients for these recipes are widely available from wholefood stores and good supermarkets. Yet, surprisingly, many of them are not a regular part of the Western diet. Quinoa with its beautiful pearly seeds, succulent wild rice, earthy buckwheat, and even the common yellow split pea, are all sadly neglected.

They are the most versatile of ingredients and I have tried to develop appetizing ways of introducing them, always with an emphasis on lightness and flavor. Delicious on their own, but naturally bland, beans, peas and grains combine well with more robust ingredients.

Fiery chilies, cilantro, lime juice, spices, tomatoes and garlic all complement the subtle flavors and mild sweetness of beans, peas and grains, while they in turn help to mellow the stronger flavors.

Nuts are another staple food which enhance dishes with their unique flavors and crunchy texture. The new season's 'wet' walnuts and the first crisp cobnuts of fall are sheer delight.

CONTENTS

POLENTA AND BASIL GRATIN

SERVES 4 TO 6

MADE FROM CORNMEAL AND INTRODUCED TO EUROPE FROM THE NEW WORLD BY COLUMBUS, POLENTA FORMED THE TRADITIONAL STAPLE DIET IN NORTHERN ITALY. IT IS CHEAP, COLORFUL AND VERSATILE – AND DEEPLY SATISFYING TO EAT.

4½ cups water	*7 ounces Fontina or mozzarella,*
1½ teaspoons salt	*sliced thinly*
2 cups yellow cornmeal	*¾ cup crumbled Gorgonzola*
8 large basil leaves, torn	*¾ cup coarsely grated Parmesan*
¼ cup pine nuts, toasted	*Pepper*
1⅔ cups Tomato Sauce	
(page 108)	

GARNISH
Chopped basil

❖ Put the water and salt in a large saucepan. Whisk in the yellow cornmeal in a stream to prevent lumps forming, and bring to a boil, stirring constantly with a wooden spoon.

❖ Lower the heat, and stir vigorously for 2-3 minutes, then cover, and simmer for 10 minutes. Continue in this way for about 40 minutes, or until the mixture pulls away from the sides of the pan.

❖ Stir in the torn basil leaves and pine nuts. Spread out the mixture in a ½-inch thick layer in a dampened shallow dish measuring about 12 x 9 inches. Let cool, and then cut into three 1½-inch strips.

❖ Lightly grease a shallow baking dish, and spread about 1 cup of the Tomato Sauce over the bottom. Arrange the polenta and slices of Fontina or Mozzarella in an overlapping layer. Sprinkle with the Gorgonzola, and spoon the remaining sauce over the top. Sprinkle with the Parmesan, and season with pepper. Bake in the oven at 400°F for 25 to 30 minutes. Garnish with basil, and serve with a green salad.

BROCCOLI AND CHILI RISOTTO

SERVES 4

TRIM THE BROCCOLI FLORETS WHERE THE STEMS MEET THE STALK. THE HEADS SHOULD BE NO MORE THAN 1 INCH ACROSS. KEEP THE STOCK SIMMERING ALL THE TIME YOU ARE COOKING THE RICE.

8 ounces broccoli florets,	*1½ cups arborio or other Italian*
blanched	*risotto rice*
2 tablespoons vegetable oil	*About 4¼ cups hot Vegetable*
3 tablespoons butter	*Stock (page 111)*
½ cup very finely chopped	*3 tablespoons freshly grated*
onion	*Parmesan*
1 to 2 fresh red chilies, seeded	*Salt and pepper*
and chopped very finely	

❖ Heat the oil and 1 tablespoon of the butter in a large non-stick skillet. Add the onion and chili, and fry gently over a medium heat for 5 to 7 minutes until the onion is translucent. Add the rice, and stir over a medium-high heat for 1 to 2 minutes until all the grains are well-coated.

❖ Pour in 1¼ cups of the hot vegetable stock. Cook over a medium-high heat, stirring constantly, until the liquid has evaporated. Add another ⅔ cup of the stock, and stir again until the liquid has evaporated. Cook for about 25 to 30 minutes, adding more stock and stirring constantly until the rice is tender, but firm to bite. It should be creamy and slightly moist, but not too runny.

❖ Remove from the heat, and stir in the reserved broccoli, Parmesan, salt and pepper, and the remaining butter.

QUINOA SALAD WITH CUCUMBER AND PISTACHIO NUTS

SERVES 4

A VERY PRETTY AND DELICATE SALAD, EVEN THOUGH MADE WITH GRAIN. THE LITTLE QUINOA GRAINS DEVELOP A BEAUTIFUL PEARLY EDGE WHEN COOKED. BULGAR WHEAT CAN BE SUBSTITUTED BUT THIS MAKES A HEAVIER DISH.

1¼ cups quinoa
1½ cups water
1½ teaspoons salt
½ cucumber
½ cup shelled pistachio nuts

1 cup halved seedless black grapes
Radicchio and lettuce leaves, to serve

DRESSING

5 teaspoons raspberry vinegar
¼ teaspoon salt
¼ teaspoon sugar

2 tablespoons olive oil
1 tablespoon pistachio oil

❖ Rinse the quinoa in several changes of water until the water becomes clear. Put in a saucepan with the water and 1 teaspoon of the salt. Bring to a boil, cover, and simmer gently for about 20 minutes until the water is absorbed.

❖ Spread out the quinoa on a clean dish cloth, and fluff with a fork to separate the grains. Let dry for 30 minutes.

❖ Peel away a broad band of skin from either side of the cucumber, then cut it into ⅛-inch slices. Taking a small pile of slices at a time, cut into matchstick strips so that each strip has a small piece of peel at either end. Cut the strips in half crosswise. Put in a strainer, sprinkle with the remaining salt, and let drain for 30 minutes.

❖ Pour boiling water over the pistachio nuts, let stand for 5 minutes, then drain and remove the skins.

❖ Put the quinoa in a bowl with the cucumber, pistachio nuts and grapes.

❖ Whisk the dressing ingredients together, and add to the bowl, tossing gently. Let stand at room temperature for at least 1 hour to allow the flavors to develop.

❖ Arrange the leaves on a shallow serving dish, and pile the quinoa salad on top.

NUT AND PEAR SALAD

SERVES 4

THIS IS BEST MADE WITH NEW SEASON NUTS – CRUNCHY WALNUTS FROM GRENOBLE, FRANCE, OR HAZELNUTS WHEN THE SHELLS ARE STILL PALE GREEN AND THE NUTMEAT STILL CRISP AND MOIST.

2 ripe juicy pears
Squeeze of lemon juice
6 tender celery stalks, leaves included
About 6 tablespoons Pear and Walnut Oil Dressing (page 109)

¾ cup roughly chopped fresh walnuts or hazelnuts
Handful of trimmed watercress or arugula, to garnish

❖ Core and dice the pears. Place in a salad bowl, and sprinkle with the lemon juice to prevent discoloration.

❖ Cut the celery into diagonal ¼-inch slices, and add to the pears. Stir in the nuts and dressing.

❖ Scatter the watercress or arugula over the salad, and serve.

GARBANZO BEAN AND EGGPLANT CASSEROLE WITH GROUND NUTS AND SEEDS

SERVES 6

A HEARTY STEW WITH RICH, EARTHY FLAVORS FROM THE GROUND NUTS AND SEEDS. SERVE WITH WARM CRUSTY BREAD OR BAKED POTATOES.

1¼ cups dried garbanzo beans, soaked overnight	1 x 14-ounce can chopped tomatoes
1 teaspoon cumin seeds	1 red bell pepper, diced
2 teaspoons coriander seeds	1 eggplant, cut into ¾-inch pieces
2 tablespoons sesame seeds	8 ounces green beans, chopped
2 teaspoons dried oregano	2½ cups Vegetable Stock (page 111)
¼ cup shelled Brazil nuts or almonds, toasted	Salt
3 tablespoons olive oil	3 tablespoons finely chopped cilantro
2 onions, chopped	Yogurt, to serve
2 cloves garlic, crushed	
½ teaspoon chili powder	

❖ Drain the garbanzo beans and cook in boiling water for 20 to 30 minutes until just soft.

❖ Dry-fry the seeds together in a heavy-based pan until the aroma rises. Add the oregano, and fry for a few more seconds.

❖ Put the seeds, oregano and nuts in a blender, and grind to a powder.

❖ Heat the oil in a heavy-based flameproof casserole. Add the onion, and fry gently over low heat for 10 minutes until translucent. Add the garlic, ground seed mixture and chilli powder. Stir-fry for 2 minutes.

❖ Add the tomatoes, garbanzo beans, remaining vegetables and the stock. Bring to a boil, season with salt, then cover, and simmer for 1 hour.

❖ Check the seasoning, adding more salt or chili powder if necessary. Stir in the cilantro, and serve with yogurt.

QUINOA PILAU WITH PEANUT SAUCE

SERVES 4

DRY-ROASTING THE QUINOA BRINGS OUT A NUTTY AROMA AND HELPS KEEP THE GRAINS LIGHT AND SEPARATE WHEN COOKED. THE SWEETNESS OF THE BUTTERNUT SQUASH HELPS BALANCE THE QUINOA'S SLIGHT BITTERNESS.

1¾ cups quinoa	5 tender celery stalks plus leaves, diced finely
4 ounces green beans	½ teaspoon salt
¼ cup/½ stick butter	Pepper
1 bay leaf	2¼ cups hot Strong Vegetable Stock (page 111)
½ onion, diced finely	Peanut Sauce (page 109), to serve
⅔ cup diced butternut squash (about 1 small squash)	

❖ Wash the quinoa thoroughly until the water becomes clear, then drain in a fine-meshed strainer. Spread out evenly in a roasting pan. Roast in the oven at 325°F for 20 minutes, stirring every 5 minutes until the moisture has evaporated, then every 2 to 3 minutes until the grains move freely and turn golden.

❖ Plunge the green beans in boiling water for 2 minutes. Drain, and cut into ¾-inch lengths.

❖ Melt the butter in a heavy-based casserole. Add the bay leaf, onion, butternut squash and celery. Simmer for 3 to 4 minutes, stirring occasionally. Stir in the quinoa, and fry for 3-4 minutes. Season with salt and pepper.

❖ Add the boiling stock, cover, and simmer over a low heat for 30 minutes, or until all the liquid has been absorbed.

❖ Stir in the green beans, and let stand for a few minutes. Serve with the peanut sauce.

RICE BALLS WITH ALFALFA AND LEEKS

SERVES 4 TO 6

THE SECRET OF GETTING RICE BALLS TO STICK TOGETHER IS TO COOK THE RICE IN MORE WATER THAN USUAL, ABOUT 2¼ CUPS FOR THE QUANTITY HERE, SO THAT IT BECOMES QUITE GLUTINOUS.

3 cups cooked rice (about 1½ cups raw)
½ cup shredded and very finely chopped leek
1 cup alfalfa sprouts
3 cloves garlic, crushed
1-inch piece fresh ginger root, chopped very finely
4 tablespoons tamari (Japanese soy sauce)
Pepper
4 tablespoons sesame seeds
4 tablespoons all-purpose flour
Peanut (or vegetable) oil, for deep frying

❖ Thoroughly mix the first 7 ingredients.
❖ With slightly wet hands, form the mixture into about 12 balls, pressing them together firmly. If you still have difficulty making the rice stick, put the mixture in a food processor, and blend for 20 seconds.
❖ Roll each ball in the sesame seeds, then in the flour.
❖ Pour about 4 inches of oil into a wok or deep pan. Heat to 350°F or until a cube of bread browns in 30 seconds.
❖ Fry the rice balls, a few at a time, for 2 to 3 minutes until brown and crisp.
❖ Drain on paper towels, and serve warm or at room temperature with Spicy Ginger and Sesame Sauce (page 108), Carrot and Cilantro Relish (page 109), and Tangy Peanut Sauce (page 106).

PEANUT AND EGG CURRY

SERVES 4

IF THE PEANUTS HAVE SKINS, TOAST THEM IN THE OVEN FOR 10 MINUTES, THEN ROLL IN A DISH CLOTH AND RUB OFF THE SKINS.

3 to 4 tablespoons dried coconut ribbons
1 teaspoon coriander seeds
½ teaspoon cumin seeds
Seeds from 6 cardamom pods
2 tablespoons sunflower oil
2 onions, sliced
1 clove garlic, crushed
1-inch piece fresh root ginger, chopped
½-1 teaspoon cayenne pepper
½ teaspoon turmeric
½ teaspoon salt
2 cups large, unsalted peanuts
1 x 14-ounce can chopped tomatoes
2 tablespoons finely chopped cilantro
1 teaspoon sugar
Pepper
1¼ cups Strong Vegetable Stock (page 111)
2 hard-cooked eggs, halved
1 tablespoon lemon juice
Cilantro leaves, to garnish
Cucumber and Mango Raita (page 110), to serve

❖ Toast the coconut ribbons in the oven at 350°F for 3 to 5 minutes until golden. Dry-fry the coriander, cumin and cardamom seeds in a small heavy pan until the aroma rises.
❖ Grind the coconut, coriander, cumin and cardamom seeds to a powder in a pestle and mortar, or coffee grinder.
❖ Heat the oil in a skillet and fry the onions gently over a low heat for 10 minutes until just colored.
❖ Add the garlic, ginger, ground spices, cayenne, turmeric and salt. Fry gently for another 5 minutes.
❖ Stir in the peanuts, tomatoes, cilantro, sugar, pepper, and stock. Bring to a boil, then simmer over a low heat, uncovered for 30 minutes, adding a little water or stock if the mixture becomes dry.
❖ Carefully stir in the hard-cooked egg halves and lemon juice, and simmer for 10 more minutes.
❖ Pour into a serving dish, and garnish with cilantro.
❖ Serve with plain, boiled rice and the Cucumber and Mango Raita.

BLACK AND WHITE CHILI WITH POLENTA CROSTINI

SERVES 6 TO 8

MAKE THE POLENTA A DAY AHEAD AND LET COOL. PUT IT
UNDER THE BROILER WHILE THE CHILI IS COOKING. IF
YOU LIKE YOUR CHILI HOT USE THE FULL AMOUNT OF
CHILI POWDER – OR MORE!

POLENTA

2¼ cups yellow cornmeal	4¼ cups pints water
1¼ teaspoons salt	Olive oil

CHILI

2 cups dried black kidney beans, soaked overnight	¼-1 teaspoon chilli powder
¾ cup dried navy beans, soaked overnight	2 x 14 ounce cans chopped tomatoes
1 teaspoon cumin seeds	3 tablespoons tomato paste
2 teaspoons coriander seeds	1 teaspoon sugar
2 teaspoons dried oregano	1 teaspoon salt
2 tablespoons olive oil	2½ cups Vegetable Stock (page 111)
2 onions, chopped	3 tablespoons chopped cilantro (or flat-leafed Italian parsley)
2 cloves garlic, chopped finely	
2 red bell peppers, cored, seeded and cut into ½-inch dice	

GARNISH
Cilantro leaves

❖ Put the polenta, salt and water in a large saucepan and stir thoroughly. Slowly bring to a boil, stirring, then pour into a greased 12 x 19-inch roasting pan. Cover with greased foil, and bake in the oven at 400°F for at least 1 hour. Let cool slightly, then turn out, and leave to become firm.

❖ When ready to make the crostini, cut the polenta into diamond-shaped slices, brush with olive oil and toast under the broiler until lightly browned on both sides.

❖ To make the chili, drain the beans, put in separate saucepans and cover with fresh water. Boil rapidly for at least 15 minutes, and then simmer for 30 to 45 minutes until just tender. Drain, and set aside.

❖ Toast the cumin and coriander seeds in a dry pan over a medium heat, shaking the pan so that they do not burn. Add the oregano, toast for 10 seconds, then remove the pan from the heat. Crush the mixture lightly with a pestle and mortar.

❖ Heat the oil in a large saucepan. Add the onion, garlic, red pepper, toasted spice mixture and chili powder. Fry gently over a medium heat for 5 minutes until the onion is soft.

❖ Add the chopped tomatoes, tomato paste, sugar, salt, beans and stock. Stir well, and bring to a boil. Cover, and simmer over a low heat for 45 minutes, stirring occasionally to prevent sticking.

❖ Stir in the chopped cilantro, and simmer for 5 more minutes.

❖ Garnish with cilantro leaves, and serve with the polenta crostini.

RICE AND PEAS WITH TOMATO ROUGAIL

SERVES 4

A MAINSTAY OF THE WEST INDIES, REFERRED TO
AS RICE AND PEAS IN JAMAICA AND HAITI, EVEN THOUGH
THE PEAS ARE IN FACT BEANS. ROUGAIL IS A HIGHLY
SPICED WEST INDIAN RELISH TRADITIONALLY SERVED
WITH RICE-BASED DISHES.

*2/3 cup dried black or red kidney
beans, soaked overnight
1/2 teaspoon salt
2 tablespoons sunflower oil
2 tablespoons finely chopped
thyme or marjoram
1 small onion, chopped finely*

*1 small red bell pepper, seeded
and diced
1 small fresh chili, seeded and
chopped
1 clove garlic, chopped finely
Pepper
1 1/3 cups white rice, rinsed*

COCONUT MILK

*3 cups shredded coconut, fresh
or dried*

*4 1/4 cups hot water or milk
and/or liquid from a fresh
coconut*

TOMATO ROUGAIL

*1 small onion, chopped
1/2-inch piece fresh root ginger,
chopped
1 fresh red chili, seeded and
chopped*

*1/4 teaspoon salt
1 tablespoon lemon juice
2 large tomatoes, peeled, seeded
and chopped*

GARNISH

*1 to 2 tablespoons toasted
coconut ribbons*

Chopped thyme

❖ Rinse and drain the beans. Put them in a saucepan with enough water to cover. Bring to a boil and boil rapidly for 15 minutes, then drain again. Cover with fresh water and simmer for about 45 to 60 minutes until tender, adding salt during the last 10 minutes of cooking time. Drain and set aside.

❖ Put the shredded coconut in a saucepan, and add the hot liquid. Cover, and simmer over a very low heat for 30 minutes.

❖ Strain through a piece of cheesecloth, twisting the cheesecloth and squeezing the pulp to extract as much juice as possible.

❖ Put all the ingredients for the rougail in a food processor and blend until smooth. Cover, and let stand at room temperature.

❖ Heat the oil in a large heavy-based saucepan, and fry the thyme or marjoram for 30 seconds. Add the onion, and fry gently for 5 minutes until translucent. Add the red bell pepper and chili, and fry for 3 minutes; then add the garlic and fry for 2 more minutes until the vegetables are soft but not colored. Season with salt and pepper.

❖ Add the beans and rice, and fry gently for 1 to 2 minutes, stirring until all the rice grains and beans are coated with oil.

❖ Pour the coconut milk over the bean mixture, stir well, and bring to a boil; then cover, and simmer for about 20 minutes until the liquid is absorbed.

❖ Transfer to a warm serving dish. Fluff with a fork, mixing in the coconut ribbons. Garnish with thyme, and serve with the tomato rougail.

CARIBBEAN BLACK BEAN SALAD WITH PALM HEARTS

SERVES 4 TO 6

SOLD IN CANS, PALM HEARTS ARE THE TENDER BUDS OF A WEST INDIAN PALM TREE. THEY HAVE A FLAVOR SIMILAR TO GLOBE ARTICHOKES AND A CRUNCHY TEXTURE.

1 cup dried black kidney or turtle beans, soaked overnight

14-ounce can palm hearts, drained

½ red bell pepper, cored, seeded and diced finely

2 scallions, green parts included, diced finely

1 fresh red or green chili, seeded and sliced finely

3 tablespoons finely chopped cilantro or parsley

DRESSING

3 tablespoons lime juice

Grated zest of 1 lime

½ teaspoon sugar

4 tablespoons olive oil

❖ Drain and rinse the beans. Cover with water, and boil rapidly for 15 minutes; then drain, rinse and cover with fresh water. Simmer for 20 to 30 minutes until just tender, adding salt during the last 10 minutes of cooking time. Drain the beans again, and put in a serving bowl.

❖ Combine the dressing ingredients, season and whisk until thick. Pour it over the beans while they are still warm, mixing well. Let the beans cool.

❖ Cut the palm hearts crosswise into ½-inch diagonal slices. Add to the beans with the remaining ingredients.

❖ Toss well, then let the salad stand at room temperature for at least 1 hour before serving.

RICE SALAD WITH SNOW PEAS AND LEMON GRASS

SERVES 4

AN ESSENTIAL FLAVORING IN SOUTHEAST ASIAN COOKERY, LEMON GRASS HAS A SUBTLE BUT DISTINCTIVE FRAGRANCE. IF YOU'RE LUCKY ENOUGH TO FIND LARGE FRESH LEMON GRASS STALKS, IT'S WORTH BUYING SOME TO FREEZE, OR THE HERB WILL KEEP FOR TWO WEEKS IN THE SALAD DRAWER OF THE REFRIGERATOR.

2 long lemon grass stalks

¾ cup long-grain rice

½ teaspoon salt

½ cup Vegetable Stock (page 111)

1 clove garlic, crushed

⅛ teaspoon ground cumin

½ dried red chili, seeded and crumbled

2 tablespoons lime juice

3 tablespoons olive oil

Salt and pepper

4 ounces snow peas or sugar snap peas, trimmed

2 scallions, green parts included, sliced finely

⅓ cup unsalted peanuts, roasted

❖ Remove and discard the tough outer stalks of the lemon grass. Chop the remaining tender stalks very finely.

❖ Wash the rice in several changes of water until the water becomes clear. Put in a small saucepan with enough water to cover by 1 inch. Add the salt and half the lemon grass. Bring to a boil, then cover and simmer over a low heat for 20 minutes until the water is absorbed.

❖ Meanwhile, put the remaining lemon grass in a small saucepan with the stock, and simmer over low heat for 10 minutes. Pour into a blender with the garlic, cumin, chili, lime juice, olive oil, salt and pepper, and purée.

❖ Put the rice in a shallow serving dish, and pour the blended lemon grass mixture over it while the rice is still warm. Fluff gently with a fork and let cool.

❖ Steam the snow peas over boiling water for 2 minutes. Drain under cold running water, and pat dry with paper towels. Slice into ¾-inch pieces, and add to the rice.

❖ Stir in the scallions and roasted peanuts. Let stand for 1 hour at room temperature before serving.

STIR-FRIED BROWN RICE WITH SHIITAKE MUSHROOMS AND SEAWEED

SERVES 4

SEAWEED IS HIGHLY VALUED IN JAPAN. TRY THE MILDER ONES, ARAME OR HIZIKI, TO START WITH.

¼ cup arame or hiziki, tightly packed

2 tablespoons tamari (Japanese soy sauce)

1 tablespoon umeboshi vinegar (or white wine vinegar)

1 teaspoon wasabi powder (optional)

2 tablespoons sunflower oil

2 teaspoons dark sesame oil

3 cloves garlic, chopped finely

1-inch piece fresh ginger root, chopped very finely

¾ cup yellow bell pepper, cut into matchstick strips

1 cup shiitake mushrooms, sliced very finely

½ cup leek (green and white parts), cut into matchstick strips

1½ cups cooked brown rice (about ¾ cup dry weight)

❖ Rinse the arame, and soak in cold water for at least 1 hour. Drain, and reserve the soaking water.

❖ Combine the tamari and umeboshi in a small bowl, then stir in the wasabi powder if using.

❖ Heat the oils in a wok or skillet. Add the garlic and ginger, and stir-fry over a high heat for 10 seconds. Add the yellow bell pepper, mushrooms, leek, arame and 2 tablespoons of the arame soaking water. Stir-fry for about 2 minutes then transfer to a bowl and keep warm.

❖ Add the rice to the wok or skillet, sprinkle with 3 tablespoons of arame soaking water, and stir-fry for 2 minutes until heated through. Stir in the tamari mixture.

❖ Return the vegetables to the pan, and stir until heated through.

TOFU AND CASHEW NUT STIR-FRY

SERVES 4

WRAP THE TOFU IN SEVERAL LAYERS OF PAPER TOWELS AND LEAVE WITH A WEIGHT ON TOP TO DRAIN FOR 30 MINUTES. IT SHOULD BE AS DRY AS POSSIBLE.

14 ounces firm tofu, drained and pressed dry

4 tablespoons hoisin sauce

1 tablespoon dry sherry

1 tablespoon soy sauce

½ teaspoon salt

Pepper

4 to 5 scallions

3 tablespoons peanut oil

3 cloves garlic, chopped finely

3 slices fresh ginger root, chopped finely

2 fresh chilies, seeded and sliced finely

2 cups shiitake mushrooms, sliced thinly

¾ cup roasted, unsalted cashew nuts

2 teaspoons dark sesame oil

❖ Cut the tofu in half horizontally, and then into ½-inch cubes. Mix together the hoisin sauce, sherry, soy sauce, salt and pepper in a bowl.

❖ Cut the scallions into three, separating the white and green parts. Cut each piece lengthwise into shreds.

❖ Heat 2 tablespoons of the peanut oil in a wok or skillet until almost smoking. Add two-thirds of the garlic and ginger, and stir-fry for 30 seconds.

❖ Add the chilies, the white part of the scallions and the mushrooms. Stir-fry for 2 minutes, then set aside.

❖ Heat the remaining oil over a high heat, and stir-fry the remaining garlic and ginger for a few seconds.

❖ Add the tofu with the hoisin sauce mixture, and stir-fry over a medium heat for 3 minutes. Return the mushroom mixture to the pan, and toss in the sauce until well coated.

❖ Stir in the cashew nuts and green scallions. Sprinkle with sesame oil and serve immediately.

FALAFEL WITH MINTED YOGURT SAUCE

SERVES 4 TO 6

COATING THE FALAFEL WITH EGG YOLK IS NOT
STRICTLY AUTHENTIC, BUT IT HELPS PREVENT THE MIXTURE
FROM FALLING APART.

*1¼ cups garbanzo beans or dried
fava beans, soaked overnight
2 teaspoons coriander seeds
1 teaspoon cumin seeds
1 onion, chopped finely
2 cloves garlic, crushed
4 tablespoons finely chopped
cilantro or parsley
4 tablespoons lemon juice*

*2 tablespoons all-purpose flour
¼ teaspoon baking powder
Salt and cayenne pepper
Beaten egg yolk
Flour for dusting
Peanut (or vegetable) oil, for
frying
Minted Yogurt Sauce
(page 107), to serve*

❖ Drain and rinse the garbanzo or fava beans. Put in a large saucepan of water. Bring to a boil, and simmer for 20-30 minutes until soft. Add salt in the last 10 minutes.

❖ Dry-fry the spices in a small, heavy pan for a few minutes until the aroma rises. Then crush in a mortar.

❖ Drain the beans, and purée in a food processor with the spices and remaining ingredients until smooth. Chill the mixture for at least 1 hour.

❖ Form into flattish cakes, about 1½ inches in diameter, pressing the mixture together firmly. Dip in beaten egg yolk, and roll in flour. Chill for 15 minutes.

❖ Pour about 4 inches of oil into a deep pan. Heat to 350°F or until a cube of bread browns in 30 seconds. Fry the falafel for about 3 minutes until golden-brown. Drain on paper towels.

❖ Stuff into warmed pita bread pockets with a spoonful of Minted Yogurt Sauce, sliced onions, shredded lettuce and lemon wedges.

LENTIL AND CHERRY TOMATO SALAD WITH GINGER DRESSING

SERVES 4

PUY LENTILS ARE BEST FOR THIS DISH AS THEY HAVE A
ROBUST, EARTHY FLAVOR. LET THE SALAD STAND AT ROOM
TEMPERATURE FOR AN HOUR OR TWO.

*1 cup Puy lentils, rinsed
Coarse sea salt
Pepper
3 scallions*

*1 cup cherry tomatoes
1 tablespoon toasted sesame seeds
½ cup plain yogurt or heavy
cream*

DRESSING

*2-inch piece fresh root ginger,
crushed in a garlic press
1 tablespoon lime or lemon juice
1 clove garlic, crushed*

*1½ teaspoons sugar
Salt and pepper
4 tablespoons olive oil
1 teaspoon dark sesame oil*

❖ Whisk together all the dressing ingredients in the order listed, and set aside.

❖ Put the lentils in a saucepan with 2½ cups of water. Bring to a boil, and simmer for 15 minutes until just tender. Drain, and transfer to a serving dish.

❖ Pour half the dressing over the lentils while they are still warm. Season generously with coarse sea salt and freshly ground pepper. Let cool.

❖ Cut the scallions, green parts included, into 1¼-inch pieces. Cut the pieces lengthwise into shreds.

❖ Stir all but 1 tablespoon of the onions into the lentils. Halve the tomatoes and add with the sesame seeds.

❖ Mix the remaining dressing with the yogurt or cream, and stir into the lentils. Garnish with the remaining onions.

CILANTRO DHAL WITH CARAMELIZED ONION RINGS

SERVES 4

TRADITIONALLY USED IN PEASE PUDDING, A DISH FROM NORTHERN ENGLAND, YELLOW SPLIT PEAS HAVE A WARM EARTHY FLAVOR WHICH COMBINES WELL WITH SPICES. ALTHOUGH NOT STRICTLY NECESSARY, SOAKING FOR AN HOUR OR TWO BEFOREHAND WILL HELP THE PEAS BREAK DOWN TO A PUREE.

1¼ cups yellow split peas, rinsed
4¼ cups pints water
10 black peppercorns
½ teaspoon coriander seeds
3 cloves
Seeds from 2 cardamom pods
2 onions
2 tablespoons sunflower oil
2 tablespoons butter
½ teaspoon mustard seeds

4 cloves garlic, crushed
1-inch piece fresh root ginger, chopped finely
½ teaspoon turmeric
½ teaspoon chili powder
2 tablespoons lemon juice
1 teaspoon salt
3 tablespoons finely chopped cilantro

GARNISH
Cilantro leaves

❖ Put the peas in a saucepan with the water. Bring to a boil, and simmer for 30 minutes until most of the liquid is absorbed and the peas are very soft.

❖ Crush the peppercorns, cilantro seeds, cloves and cardamom seeds in a mortar and set aside.

❖ Chop 1 of the onions very finely, and set aside. Cut the remaining onion into ¼-inch thick slices. Keep the rings in place by inserting 2 or 3 toothpicks from the outside to the center. Brush both sides with some of the oil, and place under a very hot broiler for 5 to 7 minutes on each side until blackened round the edges.

❖ Heat the butter and remaining oil in a pan, and fry the mustard seeds until they begin to pop. Add the chopped onion, and fry gently for 5 to 7 minutes until translucent.

❖ Add the garlic and ginger, and fry for another 2 to 3 minutes, then stir in the turmeric, chili powder and the crushed spices. Stir-fry for 2 minutes.

❖ Add the peas, stir in the lemon juice, salt and chopped cilantro, and simmer for a few minutes over a low heat. Add a little water if the mixture becomes dry.

❖ Transfer to a heated serving dish, and top with the onion rings, removing the cocktail sticks first. Garnish with cilantro leaves, and serve with yogurt.

WILD RICE AND HAZELNUT SALAD

SERVES 4

A ROBUST SALAD, WARMLY
FLAVORED WITH ORANGE, GINGER AND THYME.

1 cup wild rice, rinsed	*12 ounces young fava beans,*
1 bay leaf	*shelled (or ¾ cup frozen)*
1 strip orange zest	*4 ounces fine green beans*
Salt	*Pepper*
2 cups water	*Bitter and pungent green*
2 tablespoons finely chopped	*leaves e.g. escarole, arugula, and*
thyme	*watercress, to serve*
⅓ cup shelled hazelnuts	

❖ Place the rice in a saucepan with the bay leaf, orange zest, ½ teaspoon salt and the water. Bring to a boil; then simmer, covered, for 35 to 40 minutes until tender. The rice should still be quite chewy and not mushy. Drain, discarding the bay leaf and orange zest, and mix with the dressing and thyme while still warm.

❖ Toast the hazelnuts in the oven at 350°F for 10 minutes. Remove the skins by rolling in a clean, dry dish cloth. Chop roughly, and add to the rice.

❖ Steam the fava and green beans together over boiling water for 3 to 4 minutes until barely tender. Rinse under cold water, and pat dry with paper towels. Cut the green beans into 1-inch lengths. Stir the fava and green beans into the rice.

❖ Add salt and freshly ground pepper to taste. Let stand at room temperature to allow the flavors to develop.

❖ Arrange a bed of salad leaves on 4 serving plates, and pile the rice in the center.

CHESTNUT, CELERY AND ORANGE SOUP

SERVES 4

A ZESTY SOUP WITH HIDDEN DEPTHS OF FLAVOR. USE
EITHER 1½ POUNDS FRESH CHESTNUTS, PEELED AND
HUSKED; 12 OUNCES FROZEN CHESTNUTS; OR 6 OUNCES
DRIED CHESTNUTS, SOAKED OVERNIGHT, AND THEN
SIMMERED FOR 1½ HOURS.

¼ cup butter	*½ teaspoon ground ginger*
1 onion, chopped	*1 quart Vegetable Stock*
4 celery stalks, chopped	*(page 111)*
12 ounces prepared chestnuts	*6 tablespoons orange juice*
(see note above)	*4 tablespoons heavy cream, and*
2 x 2-inch slithers of orange zest	*chopped celery leaves or lovage,*
½ teaspoon salt	*to garnish*
½ teaspoon freshly ground	
black pepper	

❖ Melt the butter in a saucepan, and add the onion and celery. Cover, and cook together over low heat for about 5 minutes.

❖ Add the chestnuts and all the remaining ingredients except the orange juice. Cover, and simmer for 30 minutes.

❖ Pour into a food processor, and blend until smooth. Return to the pan, and add the orange juice. Reheat gently, and pour into bowls.

❖ Add a swirl of cream to each bowl, and sprinkle with chopped celery leaves or lovage.

BLACK BEAN SOUP WITH YOGURT

SERVES 4

A THICK, FILLING SOUP WITH EXCITING FLAVORS. START
MAKING IT THE DAY BEFORE YOU PLAN TO SERVE IT.

*1 cup black kidney beans,
soaked overnight
3 tablespoons olive oil
2 bay leaves
2 sprigs thyme
2 small sprigs rosemary
1 onion, chopped
4 cloves garlic, peeled and left
whole
2 celery stalks, chopped*

*1 small leek, chopped
2 carrots, chopped
1 quart Vegetable Stock
(page 111)
2 teaspoons whole black
peppercorns, crushed
2 teaspoons coriander seeds,
toasted and crushed
½ teaspoon salt
1 tablespoon lemon juice*

GARNISH
Plain yogurt | Finely chopped cilantro

❖ Drain the beans, and rinse well. Put in a saucepan with
enough water to cover. Bring to a boil, and boil rapidly for
15 minutes, then drain and rinse.

❖ Heat the oil in a large, heavy-based pan. Add the herbs,
and cook for 30 seconds to flavor the oil. Add the onion,
and fry gently for 5 minutes until translucent. Add the
garlic, celery, leek, and carrots. Cover, and cook gently for
10 minutes.

❖ Add the beans, stock, peppercorns and coriander seeds.
Bring to a boil, then simmer slowly, covered, for 1 hour
until the beans are soft, stirring occasionally.

❖ Purée thoroughly in a food processor and reheat. Season
to taste with salt and add the lemon juice.

❖ Serve in large bowls, swirl in a spoonful of yogurt and
sprinkle with chopped cilantro.

HAZELNUT AND WARM
JERUSALEM ARTICHOKE SALAD

SERVES 4

A RICHLY FLAVORED SALAD, TO MAKE IN THE FALL.
THE EARTHY TASTE OF THE ARTICHOKES COMBINES WELL
WITH THE SWEETNESS OF THE HAZELNUTS. STEAMING
CONSERVES THE FLAVOR AND HELPS PREVENT THE
SLICES FROM BREAKING UP.

*¾ cup shelled hazelnuts
1 pound Jerusalem artichokes
1 lemon
4 ounces fine green beans
2 tablespoons hazelnut oil*

*3 tablespoons finely chopped
parsley or chervil
Coarse sea salt
Pepper*

❖ Roast the hazelnuts at 350°F for 8 to 10 minutes. Rub off
the skins in a dish cloth, then chop roughly.

❖ Squeeze the juice from half the lemon into a bowl of
cold water.

❖ Peel the artichokes, removing any knobbly bits, and cut
into ¼-inch thick slices, dropping them into the lemon
water as you work.

❖ Trim the beans, and cut into ¾-inch lengths.

❖ Drain the artichokes, and steam with the beans over
boiling water for 4 to 5 minutes until just tender.

❖ Put into a serving bowl. Sprinkle with the oil and
1 tablespoon of lemon juice, and toss gently until all the
slices are coated.

❖ Add the hazelnuts and parsley or chervil. Season generously with coarse sea salt and a few twists of the pepper
grinder. Toss again gently, and serve while still warm.

STIR-FRY OF CHESTNUTS AND MUSHROOMS

SERVES 4

FRESHLY GATHERED CHESTNUTS AND MUSHROOMS MAKE
THIS A MAGIC DISH FOR A FALL EVENING. BUT IT'S STILL
WORTH MAKING WITH CULTIVATED MUSHROOMS AND
FROZEN OR DRIED CHESTNUTS. IF USING DRIED CHESTNUTS,
SOAK OVERNIGHT, SIMMER FOR 1½ HOURS IN WATER, THEN
DRAIN AND FOLLOW THE RECIPE.

6 fl oz Vegetable Stock (page 111)	*8 ounces large mushrooms*
18 ounces fresh chestnuts, peeled and husked, or 4 ounces dried, cooked as above, or 7 ounces frozen chestnuts, thawed	*2 cloves garlic, chopped very finely*
	Coarse sea salt
	Pepper
4 tablespoons olive oil	*5 tablespoons finely chopped parsley*

❖ Bring the stock to a boil, and add the chestnuts. Bring back to a boil, and simmer rapidly for 5 to 7 minutes. Drain the chestnuts, reserving the stock, and cut each one in half. Boil the stock rapidly until reduced by half, then reserve.

❖ Heat the oil in a skillet, add the mushrooms, and stir-fry for 5 minutes over medium heat. Add the chestnuts and garlic and fry for another 2 to 3 minutes.·

❖ Add the reduced stock, season generously with coarse sea salt and freshly ground pepper, and stir in the chopped parsley. Simmer for another minute or two, and serve.

ROASTED BUCKWHEAT WITH KOHLRABI

SERVES 4

USE ROASTED BUCKWHEAT (KASHA) AS IT HAS A BETTER
FLAVOR THAN THE RAW VARIETY. COATING THE
BUCKWHEAT WITH EGG KEEPS THE GRAINS SEPARATE AND
PREVENTS THEM FROM BECOMING MUSHY.

1½ cups roasted buckwheat	*1 tablespoon finely chopped dill*
1 egg, beaten	*1 teaspoon fennel seeds, toasted and crushed*
3 to 4 small kohlrabi (about 1 pound)	*Salt and pepper*
pat of butter	*⅔ cup sour cream*
2 tablespoons finely chopped parsley	*2 tablespoons lemon juice*

GARNISH

Dill leaves | Paprika

❖ Put the buckwheat in a saucepan with the beaten egg. Stir until all the grains are coated. Place over medium heat, and stir for about 1 minute until the grains are dry and separate. Break up any lumps with a fork. Add enough boiling water to cover by ½ inch. Add salt, and simmer, uncovered, for about 15 minutes until all the liquid has been absorbed. Cover, and keep warm.

❖ Meanwhile, peel the kohlrabi, and cut into ¼-inch slices. Cut each slice into 4. Simmer in salted water for 4 to 5 minutes until just tender.

❖ Drain the kohlrabi, and return to the pan. Add the butter, parsley, dill, and fennel seeds and season generously with salt and pepper. Fry gently over low heat for a minute or two, then stir in the sour cream and lemon juice, and heat through.

❖ Transfer the buckwheat to a warmed serving dish, and top with the kohlrabi mixture. Sprinkle with paprika, and garnish with dill leaves.

RED CABBAGE WITH A CRISP NUT STUFFING

A DISH OF VIBRANT COLOR AND CRUNCHY TEXTURE -
PERFECT FOR A WINTER EVENING MEAL. IT MAKES A
CHANGE FROM THE USUAL WAY OF COOKING RED CABBAGE
WITH VINEGAR, APPLES AND ONIONS.

1 red cabbage (about 2¼ pounds)	*1¼ cups thinly sliced mushrooms*
4 tablespoons olive oil	*3 cloves garlic, chopped finely*
¼ cup butter	*1 tablespoon dried herbes de Provence or mixed herbs*
2 cups wholewheat bread crumbs	*Grated zest of ½ lemon*
1½ cups chopped mixed nuts (Brazil nuts, cashews, walnuts, and peanuts)	*½ teaspoon salt*
	Pepper
1 onion, chopped finely	*1¼ cups Vegetable Stock (page 111)*

TO SERVE
Roasted Red Bell Pepper Sauce (page 106) or Tomato Sauce (page 108)

❖ Cut off 1½ inches from the base of the cabbage, and carefully peel away 6 to 8 outer leaves. Plunge the leaves into a large saucepan of boiling water for 2 to 3 minutes. Drain under cold running water, and pat dry with paper towels. Using a small, sharp knife, shave away some of the base of the thick stalk so that the leaves are easier to bend.

❖ Cut the center of the cabbage in half. Discard one piece for use in another dish. Slice the remaining cabbage lengthwise into 4, and cut out the thick central stalk. Cut the cabbage crosswise into shreds.

❖ To make the stuffing, heat 1 tablespoon of the oil and half the butter in a skillet. Fry the breadcrumbs and nuts together for 3 to 4 minutes over medium heat until the crumbs are crisp. Put the mixture in a bowl, and wipe out the pan.

❖ Heat the remaining oil and 1 tablespoon of the butter and fry the onion gently for a few minutes over a medium heat until translucent. Add the mushrooms and shredded cabbage, and fry for 5 minutes. Stir in the garlic and herbs, and fry for another 2 minutes. Add to the nut mixture in the bowl.

❖ Stir in the lemon zest, salt, a generous amount of freshly ground pepper and ⅔ cup of the stock.

❖ Arrange the leaves around the edge of a shallow, oven-proof dish, about 8½ inches in diameter, overlapping them so that there are no gaps. Pile the stuffing in the center, dot with the remaining butter, and fold over the tops of the leaves. Pour the remaining stock around the outside of the leaves.

❖ Cover the dish tightly with a double thickness of foil. Bake for 45 minutes at 350°F. Serve in wedges with the sauce.

GARBANZO BEAN AND EGGPLANT DIP

SERVES 4

TO EXTRACT MAXIMUM JUICE
FROM THE LIME, ROLL IT ON A HARD SURFACE.

2 small eggplants
½ cup dried garbanzo beans,
soaked overnight
¼ teaspoon salt
6 tablespoons yogurt, strained
through a cheesecloth

Grated zest of ½ lime
2 tablespoons lime juice
1 clove garlic, crushed
2 tablespoons olive oil
Pinch of cayenne
Black olives and cayenne pepper

❖ Grill the eggplants for 15 to 20 minutes, turning occasionally, until charred. Let cool slightly, then remove the skin. Squeeze out the bitter juices, and leave to drain.
❖ Put the garbanzo beans in a large saucepan of water. Bring to a boil, and simmer for about 20 minutes until soft. Add salt during the last 10 minutes of cooking time.
❖ Drain and purée with the eggplants and remaining ingredients, until smooth. Transfer to a serving bowl, and garnish with black olives and cayenne pepper.

YELLOW SPLIT PEA AND WALNUT PUREE

SERVES 4

A QUICKLY MADE DIP. SERVE IT WITH
BLUE CORN TORTILLA CHIPS OR WARM PITA BREAD.

¾ cup yellow split peas, rinsed
and drained
⅓ cup shelled walnuts, chopped
roughly
5 tablespoons yogurt, strained
through a cheesecloth
1 clove garlic, crushed

2 scallions, green part included,
chopped
1 tablespoon lemon juice
1 tablespoon olive oil
Salt and pepper
Walnut pieces and chopped
scallion tops, to garnish

❖ Put the split peas in a saucepan with enough water to cover by 1 inch. Bring to a boil, then simmer, stirring occasionally, for 20 to 25 minutes until the liquid is absorbed and the split peas are soft.
❖ Purée in a food processor with all the remaining ingredients until smooth, adding more lemon juice or salt and pepper if necessary.
❖ Transfer to a serving bowl, and garnish with a few walnut pieces and chopped scallion tops.

LENTIL, MINT AND LEMON DIP

SERVES 4

PUY LENTILS HAVE THE BEST FLAVOR BUT YOU
CAN USE ORDINARY BROWN OR GREEN LENTILS INSTEAD.

⅔ cups Puy lentils, soaked
overnight
1 teaspoon cumin seeds, toasted
and crushed
1 clove garlic, crushed

Grated zest of 1 lemon
3 tablespoons lemon juice
3 tablespoons olive oil
4 tablespoons chopped mint
Salt and pepper

❖ Drain the soaked lentils, and rinse. Put them in a saucepan with 1¼ cups water. Bring to a boil, then simmer for 5 minutes until soft. Drain again.
❖ Put the lentils in a food processor with the remaining ingredients, and process until smooth. Add more lemon juice, salt and pepper if necessary.
❖ Transfer to a serving bowl, and garnish with a twist of lemon and a mint sprig.

PASTA, PASTRY, PANCAKES AND BREADS

Various types of dough can be made from flour and water or eggs. The recipes in this chapter mainly use wheat flour, although some use garbanzo or garam flour, rice flour, cornmeal or polenta. These all-time staples, combined with vegetables, pulses or dairy products, create satisfying dishes which form the basis of countless vegetarian meals.

Pasta is one of the most comforting of foods – easily made and cooked. There's nothing to beat homemade pasta, using flour moistened with eggs and a little oil, kneaded until elastic, then rolled out. Of the commercial dried pastas, I find the best brands are Italian. Cook pasta in plenty of boiling water – about 5 quarts for every 1 pound of pasta. Cooking times can only be approximate so you need to test to see if it's ready. The pasta should be tender but still with some bite to it.

Meltingly crisp golden pastry makes a very appealing foil to a variety of fillings – colorful chunks of broiled or stir-fried vegetables, or puffy, egg-based custards seasoned with herbs. Pastry dishes are best accompanied by a crisp salad, or plainly cooked vegetables of a contrasting type or color to the filling.

Pancakes and tortillas are great for mopping up sauces and dips, or they can be filled with tasty well-seasoned morsels of freshly cooked food or leftovers. No meal is complete without bread. Any doubts you have about making your own will soon disappear once you experience the satisfaction of transforming what can be a sticky mess into a silky smooth, elastic dough – and eating the results.

CONTENTS

NOODLES WITH BROILED MARINATED VEGETABLES

SERVES 4

THIS MARINADE IS RATHER LIKE A
PESTO SAUCE WITH ORIENTAL UNDERTONES.

2 small red onions, unpeeled	1 eggplant
2 heads of purple garlic	1 large yellow bell pepper, seeded
4 small zucchini	Olive oil for brushing
2 small plump heads of endive	4 ounces egg vermicelli

MARINADE

Handful of torn basil leaves	1 fresh chili, seeded and chopped
Handful of fennel fronds	Juice and finely grated zest
Handful of cilantro, trimmed and chopped roughly	of 1 lime
	8 tablespoons olive oil
1-inch piece fresh ginger root, chopped finely	½ cup peanuts, toasted
	1 teaspoon raw brown sugar
2 large cloves garlic, chopped	½ teaspoon salt

❖ Purée the marinade ingredients in a blender until smooth.

❖ Cut the onions and garlic in half crosswise and the zucchini and endive lengthwise. Cut the yellow bell pepper into quarters and slice the eggplant lengthwise.

❖ Place the vegetables in a single layer in a dish. Brush with the marinade, and sprinkle with olive oil. Cover, and marinate for at least 2 hours, preferably overnight.

❖ Remove the vegetables, scraping off and reserving the marinade, and place on a rack over medium-hot coals or under a preheated broiler. Cook for 10 to 15 minutes, brushing with oil and turning, until tender and beginning to blacken.

❖ Meanwhile, cook the vermicelli. Drain, return to the pan, and toss with the reserved marinade. Arrange a nest of vermicelli on four plates, and top with a selection of broiled vegetables.

SPICED ONION BREAD

MAKES 1 LOAF

ADAPTED FROM AN ETHIOPIAN RECIPE, A SLICE OF THIS
ROBUSTLY FLAVORED LOAF IS ALMOST A MEAL IN ITSELF.
DELICIOUS STILL WARM FROM THE OVEN AND THICKLY
SPREAD WITH UNSALTED BUTTER.

1 x ¼-ounce envelope active dry yeast	1 teaspoon sesame seeds
	1½ teaspoons salt
1 teaspoon brown sugar	¾ teaspoon coarsely ground
1 cup tepid (105°F) water	black pepper
1 small onion, chopped finely	¼ teaspoon cayenne
1 clove garlic, chopped finely	2 teaspoons grated fresh ginger
6 tablespoons butter	root
2 teaspoons cumin seeds	4 cups strong white flour
2 teaspoons coriander seeds	Melted butter, to glaze
1 teaspoon fenugreek seeds	

❖ Mix the yeast, sugar and water until frothy. Fry the onion and garlic in 2 tablespoons of the butter until the onion is translucent. Dry-fry the seeds for a few minutes then grind to a powder.

❖ Melt the remaining butter. Stir in the seeds, ginger and onion. Add 1 cup of the flour, then whisk in the yeast liquid. Cover, and leave in a warm place for 1 hour.

❖ Add the remaining flour, and knead for 15 minutes. Place in an oiled bowl, cover, and let stand in a warm place for 1 to 2 hours until doubled in size. Punch down, and form into a loaf shape. Place on a floured baking sheet, and cut a cross in the center. Let rise for 20 minutes.

❖ Bake at 350°F for 50 to 60 minutes until the bottom sounds hollow when tapped. Brush with melted butter while still warm.

FUSILLI WITH CILANTRO PESTO

SERVES 4

CILANTRO INSTEAD OF BASIL GIVES A NEW SLANT TO PESTO. PECORINO SARDO CHEESE IS LESS SALTY THAN THE MORE WIDELY AVAILABLE ROMANO TYPE. IF YOU USE ROMANO, REDUCE THE QUANTITY TO TASTE.

1 cup trimmed cilantro	Black pepper
4 tablespoons extra virgin olive oil	¼ cup freshly grated Parmesan
1 clove garlic, chopped finely	6 teaspoons finely grated Pecorino Sardo cheese
¼ cup pine nuts, toasted	8 ounces young green beans, trimmed
2 teaspoons lime juice	9 ounces fusilli
Coarse sea salt	

❖ Put the cilantro, olive oil, garlic, pine nuts and lime juice in a food processor with a generous pinch of sea salt and several grindings of black pepper. Blend until smooth.

❖ Transfer to a bowl, and whisk in the cheeses.

❖ Plunge the beans into boiling salted water for 3 minutes. Drain, chop into 1-inch lengths, and keep warm.

❖ Boil the fusilli in salted water until just tender. Drain and toss with the beans and cilantro pesto. Serve immediately with a cherry tomato salad.

ORIENTAL NOODLE SALAD WITH CUCUMBER, MUSHROOM AND SEAWEED

SERVES 6

A DRAMATIC SALAD WITH JUST A HINT OF SEAWEED. IT'S IMPORTANT TO USE TAMARI (JAPANESE SOY SAUCE) AS ORDINARY SOY SAUCE IS TOO HARSH. YOU CAN BUY TAMARI AND SEAWEED FROM GOOD HEALTH FOOD STORES.

18 yellow oyster mushrooms	5 ounces Chinese cellophane rice noodles
3 tablespoons vegetable oil	1 tablespoon dark sesame oil
1 cup tightly packed dried arame (seaweed), soaked for 2 hours	½ cucumber, cut into matchstick strips
2 tablespoons tamari (Japanese soy sauce)	

DRESSING

4 tablespoons toasted sesame seeds	2 teaspoons rice vinegar
2 tablespoons tamari	1½ teaspoons sugar
1 tablespoon sunflower oil	½ teaspoon salt
½ teaspoon dark sesame oil	⅛ teaspoon pepper

❖ Fry the mushrooms gently in 2 tablespoons of the oil for 5 minutes. Drain on paper towels, and leave to cool.

❖ Drain the arame, reserving the soaking water, and add to the pan with the remaining oil. Stir-fry for 5 minutes. Add the tamari and all but 4 tablespoons of soaking water. Simmer until the liquid has almost evaporated. Spread out on a plate to cool.

❖ Cook the noodles as directed on the package. Rinse and drain thoroughly, then toss in a bowl with the sesame oil.

❖ To make the dressing, grind 3 tablespoons of the sesame seeds to a powder in a blender. Add to the remaining ingredients with the arame soaking water. Whisk until thick.

❖ Divide the noodles between six plates, spreading them out in a circle. Make a circle of arame in the center, and pour some dressing over the arame. Top with a pile of cucumber strips and place three mushrooms around the edge. Sprinkle with the remaining whole sesame seeds and serve.

HERBED CORNMEAL TARTLETS WITH ASPARAGUS AND MUSHROOMS

SERVES 8

THE CORNMEAL GIVES THE PASTRY A PLEASANTLY GRITTY TEXTURE WHICH CONTRASTS WELL WITH THE VEGETABLES. SAVE TIME AND DISH-WASHING BY STEAMING THE VEGETABLES TOGETHER. PUT THE ASPARAGUS AT THE BOTTOM OF THE STEAMER BASKET, THEN THE BABY CORN, WITH THE CARROTS ON TOP.

DOUGH

1½ cups self-rising flour
1 cup yellow cornmeal
Salt
Cayenne pepper

2 tablespoons finely chopped mixed herbs e.g. thyme, oregano, lovage, hyssop, savory
½ cup butter
4 tablespoons cold water

FILLING

16 asparagus stalks, trimmed and peeled
8 baby corn ears
½ cup thinly sliced carrot
2 cups thinly sliced small mushrooms
1 tablespoon sunflower oil
Salt and pepper

1 cup Vegetable Stock (page 111)
2 teaspoons cornstarch, blended to a paste with a little stock
2 tablespoons finely chopped chives
1½ teaspoons lemon juice

❖ Sift the flour and cornmeal into a mixing bowl with a pinch of salt and cayenne. Add the herbs, then rub in the butter until the mixture resembles fine bread crumbs. Stir in the water to form a smooth dough. Cover with plastic wrap, and chill for 30 minutes.

❖ Roll out the dough to a ¼-inch thickness. Cut out eight 5-inch circles, using the trimmings to make up the required amount. Use to line 8 fluted 4-inch diameter greased tartlet pans, pressing the dough well into the edges. Place on a baking sheet and bake at 400°F for 20 minutes until slightly golden.

❖ Meanwhile, steam the asparagus, baby corn and carrots over boiling water for 5 minutes until only just tender. Reserve the asparagus tips as a garnish, and cut the stalks and the corn into ½-inch slices.

❖ Stir-fry the mushrooms in the oil for 5 minutes over medium heat, seasoning with salt and pepper.

❖ Add the stock, and bring to a boil. Add the cornstarch paste, and stir until thickened. Add the chives and lemon juice, then gently stir in the asparagus stalks, sweetcorn and carrots. Simmer for 1 minute to heat through. Check the seasoning.

❖ Spoon the mixture into the tartlet shells, and garnish with the reserved asparagus tips. Serve immediately.

ITALIAN VEGETABLE PIES

SERVES 8

SWISS CHARD STEMS ARE A VEGETABLE IN THEIR OWN RIGHT. CUT THEM FROM THE LEAVES AND STIR-FRY WITH THE FAVA BEANS. IF YOU CAN'T OBTAIN CHARD, USE HALF THE QUANTITY OF SPINACH WITH ABOUT 1 POUND CHOPPED CELERY OR ASPARAGUS STEMS.

DOUGH

3 cups all-purpose flour	2 tablespoons olive oil
1½ teaspoons salt	9 tablespoons cold water
1 egg	beaten egg yolk, to glaze

FILLING

2 pounds Swiss chard	2 tablespoons finely chopped
1 tablespoon olive oil	flat-leafed Italian parsley
¼ cup/½ stick butter	2 tablespoons finely chopped
1 clove garlic, chopped finely	savory or thyme
2 shallots, chopped finely	Salt and pepper
12 ounces frozen fava beans,	2 eggs , beaten
thawed	4 tablespoons freshly grated
	Parmesan

❖ Sift the flour and salt into a large bowl. Make a well in the center, and add the egg, oil and water. Mix with a wooden spoon, gradually drawing in the flour. Knead briefly to form a smooth dough. Cover with plastic wrap, and chill for at least 1 hour.

❖ Cook the Swiss chard leaves in a very little salted water for 5 minutes. Drain, and when cool enough to handle, squeeze out as much moisture as possible. Chop roughly.

❖ Trim the stalks from the chard leaves, slice into 1-inch pieces and reserve.

❖ Heat the oil and butter in a heavy-based saucepan and fry the garlic and shallots gently over low heat for 1 minute. Add the chard stems, fava beans, parsley and savory, and stir-fry for another minute. Stir in the cooked Swiss chard leaves, and season to taste. Stir over a medium-low heat for 1 to 2 minutes, until well mixed. Let cool slightly, then stir in the eggs and Parmesan.

❖ Divide the dough into eight, and then divide each piece in two, one piece larger than the other.

❖ Roll each larger piece into a 7-inch circle, cutting around a plate to neaten the edges. Use to line eight 4-inch dough rings or pie pans, leaving the dough to overlap the edge of the ring.

❖ Pile the filling into the dough bases, then gather up the overlapping dough to cover the filling partially. The dough should come away from the edges of the ring to make a ball shape. Moisten the edges with water.

❖ Roll the smaller pieces of dough into 3½-inch circles, and place on top of the bases. Brush with beaten egg yolk to glaze. Prick the tops with a fork.

❖ Bake at 375°F for 30 minutes, or until golden. Serve hot or at room temperature.

ROASTED ARTICHOKE, EGGPLANT, RED BELL PEPPER AND GOAT CHEESE PIZZA

SERVES 4

THE CHILI-FLAVORED OIL AND ROASTED GARLIC GIVES THESE TOMATO-FREE PIZZAS ADDED ZEST.

6 oil-cured artichokes, quartered lengthwise
2 small eggplants, sliced thinly
2 red bell peppers, halved and seeded
4 large cloves garlic, unpeeled
½ teaspoon chili powder

7 tablespoons olive oil
Pizza Dough (page 110)
1¼ cups crumbled dry goat cheese
4 ounces mozzarella cheese, sliced
A few basil leaves, torn
Salt and pepper

❖ Place the artichokes, eggplant slices, bell peppers and garlic on an oiled baking sheet. Combine the chili powder and olive oil, and use a little to brush the eggplant slices. Reserve the rest.

❖ Bake at 400°F for 20 minutes, turning the eggplants and brushing with oil.

❖ Remove the skins from the bell pepper and garlic. Slice the peppers into matchstick strips, and mash the garlic.

❖ Divide the pizza dough into four balls. Roll each ball to flatten slightly. On a floured surface, slap and stretch each piece to form a 8-inch circle. Place on floured baking sheets.

❖ Brush each circle with the remaining chili and oil mixture. Smear with the garlic. Arrange the artichokes, eggplant slices and bell peppers on top. Add the cheeses and basil. Sprinkle with a little olive oil and season with salt and pepper. Bake at 475°F for about 15 to 20 minutes until the cheese is bubbling.

MUSHROOM, SAGE AND RICOTTA CANNELLONI WITH RED PEPPER SAUCE

SERVES 4

IT'S EASIER TO USE FLAT SHEETS OF LASAGNE RATHER THAN TUBES. ROLL THEM AROUND THE STUFFING AND BAKE SEAM-SIDE DOWN. IT TASTES BEST OF ALL MADE WITH HOMEMADE PASTA.

4 tablespoons olive oil
1¼ cups flat cap mushrooms, chopped
14 ounces ricotta cheese
2 tablespoons pine nuts, toasted
2 tablespoons sage, chopped finely

Salt and pepper
8 lasagne sheets, cooked
Roasted Red Bell Pepper Sauce (page 106)
2 tablespoons freshly grated Parmesan

❖ Heat the oil in a pan, and stir-fry the mushrooms for 5 minutes until the moisture has evaporated. Let cool.

❖ Mix the ricotta with the mushrooms, pine nuts and sage. Season to taste.

❖ Place some of the mixture down the center of each lasagne sheet, rolling them into tubes. Reheat the sauce, and pour a little into the base of a greased ovenproof dish. Add the tubes, seam-side down, and pour over the remaining sauce. Sprinkle with the Parmesan, cover with foil, and bake at 350°F for 20 to 30 minutes, until heated through.

FARFALLE WITH FAVA BEANS AND GOAT CHEESE

SERVES 6

THE SUBTLE FLAVOR OF SAVORY IS PERFECT WITH FAVA
BEANS, BUT YOU COULD USE THYME INSTEAD. THE DISH IS
FAIRLY RICH SO SERVE IT WITH A CRISP SALAD OF PUNGENT
AND BITTER LEAVES, SUCH AS ESCAROLE, BATAVIA,
ARUGULA, WATERCRESS, SORREL AND CHICORY.

2 pounds young fava beans, shelled
10 ounces goat cheese
3 tablespoons finely chopped savory
1 tablespoon finely chopped parsley

3 tablespoons extra virgin olive oil
12 ounces farfalle
2 tablespoons butter
1 clove garlic, chopped finely
Salt and pepper

GARNISH
Savory sprigs

❖ Blanch the beans for 2 minutes in a large saucepan of boiling water. Drain under cold running water. Peel away the tough outer skins.

❖ Beat the cheese with 2 tablespoons of the savory, the parsley, olive oil, salt and pepper.

❖ Boil the pasta in salted water until just cooked.

❖ Meanwhile, heat the butter in a small pan, and fry the garlic and remaining savory gently for 1 minute. Add the fava beans and heat through. Season with salt and pepper.

❖ Drain the pasta, and return to the pan. Stir in the cheese mixture. Transfer to a heated serving dish and scatter the beans on top. Garnish with savory sprigs.

BROILED VEGETABLES IN FILO FLOWERS

SERVES 6

SERVE WARM AS A STARTER. MUSHROOMS AND EGGPLANTS
WOULD ALSO BE GOOD VEGETABLES TO USE.

4 sheets filo pastry, 18 x 12 inches
Olive oil for brushing
2 each small red and yellow bell peppers, cored, seeded and halved

2 small zucchini, halved lengthwise
3 baby artichokes bottled in oil, halved lengthwise
Salt and pepper

GARNISH
Shavings of fresh Parmesan | *Flat-leafed Italian parsley*

❖ Lightly brush six ¾-cup ramekins with oil.

❖ Cut the filo into 24 x 6-inch squares, and cover with a damp dish cloth. Taking 4 squares at a time, brush each one with oil. Place 1 square on top of the next, twisting them so the corners are offset. Place in a ramekin, pressing down. Repeat with the remaining squares.

❖ Bake at 375°F for 15 to 20 minutes until evenly browned. Carefully remove from the ramekins, place on a wire rack, and keep warm.

❖ Meanwhile, brush the vegetables with oil, and place skin side uppermost under a hot broiler for 10 to 15 minutes until they begin to blacken.

❖ Remove the skins from the bell peppers, then chop all the vegetables into bite-sized pieces.

❖ Fill each pastry case with pieces of vegetable. Season to taste, and drizzle with a little olive oil.

❖ Garnish with Parmesan shavings and a parsley sprig.

SWISS CHARD AND CHEESE FILO PIE

SERVES 8

IF THE SWISS CHARD IS YOUNG, COOK THE STEMS WITH THE
LEAVES. OTHERWISE CUT AWAY THE STEMS AND DISCARD
THEM. YOU CAN USE SPINACH INSTEAD OF CHARD.

2 pounds Swiss chard or spinach, lightly cooked and drained
¼ cup/½ stick butter
2 leeks, halved lengthwise and thinly sliced
2 cloves garlic, finely chopped
2 tablespoons finely chopped herbs e.g. rosemary, thyme, marjoram

2 teaspoons green peppercorns
Grated zest of 1 orange
Salt
8 ounces goat cheese
1 cup ricotta or cottage cheese
2 eggs, beaten
12 sheets filo pastry
Olive oil for brushing
½ cup pine nuts, toasted

❖ Squeeze as much liquid as possible from the Swiss chard, chop roughly and set aside.
❖ Melt the butter in a pan, and fry the leeks gently for 2 to 3 minutes over medium heat, then add the garlic, herbs, peppercorns, orange zest and salt. Fry for 2 to 3 minutes.
❖ Remove to a bowl, and combine with the Swiss chard, cheeses and eggs. Season with more salt if necessary.
❖ Place 1 sheet of filo in the bottom of a greased oven-proof dish measuring 9 x 12-inches, trimming the filo to size if necessary. Brush with oil, and sprinkle with a few pine nuts. Add 5 more sheets of filo, brushing each lightly with oil and scattering pine nuts between the layers.
❖ Pour the filling into the dish, and level the surface. Cover with the remaining filo sheets, brushing them with oil and sprinkling with pine nuts. With a sharp knife cut through all the layers to make 3-inch diamonds. Bake at 400°F for 40 to 50 minutes until browned and crisp.

FETTUCCINE WITH MUSHROOM AND HERB SAUCE

SERVES 4

FRESH MORELS, OR EVEN DRIED OR BOTTLED ONES,
MAKE THIS DISH OUT OF THIS WORLD. BUT IT'S STILL
PRETTY GOOD WITH A MIXTURE OF OTHER WILD OR
CULTIVATED MUSHROOMS.

9 ounces assorted mushrooms (e.g. morels, crimini, cap, shiitake, oyster), chopped
4 tablespoons extra virgin olive oil
2 cloves garlic, chopped finely
2 tablespoons finely chopped flat-leafed parsley
1 tablespoon chopped lovage

1 tablespoon finely chopped chives
1 tablespoon lemon juice
Salt and pepper
12 ounces fresh fettuccine
1½ cups whipping cream
½ cup pine nuts, toasted
3 tablespoons basil leaves, torn

❖ Stir-fry the mushrooms over medium heat in the oil for 5 minutes until most of the liquid has evaporated. Add the garlic, parsley, lovage, chives, lemon juice, salt and pepper, and stir-fry for another minute or two.
❖ Meanwhile, boil the fettuccine in a large pan of salted water for about 4 minutes, until tender but firm to bite. Drain, and return to the pan.
❖ Stir in the cream, pine nuts, basil and several grindings of black pepper. Transfer to a heated serving dish, and scatter the mushrooms on top.

TOMATO AND OLIVE BREAD

MAKES 2 LOAVES

TOMATO PASTE TURNS THE DOUGH INTO A PINK STICKY MESS. JUST KEEP KNEADING WITH FLOURED HANDS AND IT WILL EVENTUALLY BECOME SPRINGY AGAIN. SPRAYING WITH WATER DURING BAKING GIVES THE LOAF A LOVELY CRISP CRUST.

6 cups white bread flour
1½ teaspoons salt
1½ teaspoons sugar
¼-ounce envelope quick-rising active yeast
1 tablespoon olive oil

1¾ cups tepid (105°F) water
6 tablespoons tomato paste
20 oil-cured black olives, pitted and halved
¼ cup pumpkin seeds
Flour for dusting

❖ Sift the flour, salt, sugar and yeast in a large bowl. Make a well in the center, and stir in the oil and water gradually to form a soft dough. Knead for at least 15 minutes until smooth and springy.
❖ Transfer to a large oiled bowl, and cover with plastic wrap. Let rise in a warm place for 1 to 2 hours until doubled in size.
❖ Flatten the risen dough, and spread the tomato paste, olives and pumpkin seeds over it. Dust with flour, roll up, and knead again until smooth.
❖ Divide the dough in half, and place in two greased and floured loaf tins. Dust with flour, cover, and let rise for 45 to 60 minutes until doubled in size.
❖ Bake at 400°F for 40 to 45 minutes, spraying with water 3 times during the first 10 minutes of cooking.

RICOTTA AND BASIL TART WITH SUN-DRIED TOMATOES AND OLIVES

SERVES 6

A LIGHT-TEXTURED TART WITH A RICH PASTRY SHELL. THE PARMESAN CHEESE AND OLIVES ARE QUITE SALTY SO YOU WILL NOT NEED TO ADD ANY EXTRA TO THE FILLING.

PASTRY

1½ cups all-purpose flour
½ teaspoon salt
½ cup butter

1 egg yolk
1 tablespoon cold water

FILLING

1 cup torn basil leaves
2 tablespoons olive oil
12 ounces ricotta cheese
3 tablespoons grated Parmesan
3 eggs

5 tablespoons whipping cream
¼ cup chopped, oil-cured sun-dried tomatoes, chopped
10 oil-cured black olives, pitted and chopped

❖ Sift the flour and salt into a bowl, and rub in the butter. Mix in the egg yolk and water to form a smooth dough. Cover with plastic wrap and chill for 30 minutes.
❖ Roll out the dough thinly and use to line a 9½-10-inch metal tart pan. Line the pan with foil and baking beans, and bake "blind" at 400°F for 8 minutes. Remove the foil and beans, and bake for another 5 to 7 minutes until the edges are just golden. Let cool.
❖ Put the basil, oil and cheeses in a food processor. Season with pepper and process until just mixed. Add the eggs and cream, and process again. Stir in the sun-dried tomatoes and olives, but do not process.
❖ Pour the mixture into the pie shell, and bake at 400°F for 40 to 45 minutes until set. Serve hot or at room temperature.

GARBANZO BEAN CREPES

MAKES 8

GARBANZO BEAN FLOUR, OR GRAM FLOUR AS IT IS OFTEN CALLED, MAKES BEAUTIFUL LACY CREPE-LIKE PANCAKES, BUT THEY NEED CAREFUL HANDLING. USE A LITTLE MORE OIL THAN USUAL, AND MAKE SURE IT IS REALLY HOT. THE PANCAKES ARE QUITE PUNGENT BECAUSE OF THE CHILIES, SO A COOLING YOGURT-BASED SAUCE IS A WELCOME ACCOMPANIMENT.

2 cups garbanzo bean flour
2 teaspoons salt
2 teaspoons black sesame seeds
1 teaspoon turmeric
¼ teaspoon ground black pepper

2 fresh green chilies, seeded and chopped finely
2½ cups pint cold water
Peanut (or vegetable) oil for frying

TO SERVE
A yogurt-based sauce e.g.:
Cilantro Sauce (page 107)
Minted Yogurt Sauce (page 107)

Cucumber and Mango Raita (page 109)

❖ Sift the flour and salt into a bowl, and combine with the spices and chilies. Make a well in the center, and whisk in the water gradually, drawing in the flour from the edge, until you have a smooth batter. Cover, and let stand for 30 minutes. Whisk again just before using.

❖ Heat 2 to 3 teaspoons of oil in a heavy-based non-stick 8 to 9-inch skillet until just smoking.

❖ Pour in a ladleful of batter with a circular motion so that the batter is distributed right to the edges. Smooth the top immediately with a spatula, spreading the batter evenly. Lift the edge when it has just set, and let any surplus batter run underneath. Cook over a fairly high heat for about 50 seconds on each side. Interleave each cooked pancake with a paper towel, cover with a plate, and keep warm while you cook the rest.

❖ Fold the pancakes carefully into four, and serve with a yogurt-based sauce.

THREE-CHEESE CALZONI

SERVES 4 TO 6

CALZONI ARE ITALIAN TURNOVERS MADE WITH VERY THIN PIZZA DOUGH. THEY CAN BE BAKED IN THE OVEN BUT FRYING MAKES THEM PUFFY AND CRISP. SERVE AS A STARTER OR WITH A TOMATO SAUCE AS A MAIN COURSE.

Pizza Dough (page 110)

FILLING
1 cup ricotta cheese, strained
1¼ cups diced mozzarella cheese,
½ cup freshly grated Parmesan

1 egg, lightly beaten
2 large tomatoes, skinned, seeded and chopped
¼ teaspoon black pepper
3 tablespoons chopped basil

❖ Combine the filling ingredients and set aside.

❖ Place the risen pizza dough on a floured surface, and knead for a few minutes. Divide into 12 pieces, and roll each into a ball. Roll out to a ⅛-inch thick circle, neatening the edges by cutting around an upturned bowl.

❖ Place a scant 2 tablespoons of filling on half of the circle, leaving a narrow border. Moisten the edge, fold over, and seal. Let stand in a warm place for 15 minutes.

❖ Heat 1-inch of peanut or vegetable oil in a large skillet until very hot. Fry a few calzoni at a time for 2 to 3 minutes on each side until golden-brown. Keep warm in a hot oven while you fry the rest. Serve immediately.

ZUCCHINI AND CILANTRO GOUGERE

SERVES 4

A SPECTACULARLY COLORFUL DISH WHICH
IS SIMPLE TO PREPARE. USE SMALL GREEN ZUCCHINI
ABOUT 5-INCHES LONG.

CHOUX PASTRY

6 tablespoons butter	1 cup all-purpose flour
¾ cup water	2 eggs
¼ teaspoon salt	1 egg white
Cayenne pepper	2 ounces Red Leicester cheese,
½ teaspoon cumin seeds, toasted	grated

FILLING

2 tablespoons butter	2 teaspoons lemon juice
2 shallots, chopped finely	1 tablespoon finely chopped
2 cloves garlic, chopped finely	cilantro
1½ tablespoons all-purpose	Salt and pepper
flour	6 small zucchini, trimmed and
¼ teaspoon turmeric	sliced lengthwise into thin strips
1¼ cups milk	

❖ Put the butter, water, salt, cayenne and cumin in a saucepan, and stir until the butter has melted. Bring just to a boil, and remove from the heat. Add the flour all at once, and beat vigorously with a wooden spoon until the mixture pulls away from the sides of the pan. Beat for 1 minute over a very low heat, then let cool slightly.

❖ Lightly beat the eggs and egg white together. Gradually beat into the mixture with the cheese until very smooth and glossy.

❖ Using a plain ½-inch tip, pipe 2 circles of mixture, one on top of the other, round the edge of four 5½-inch diameter greased ovenproof dishes. Bake at 425°F for about 25 minutes until golden and puffed.

❖ Meanwhile, melt the butter in a saucepan, and fry the shallots and garlic gently over low heat for 3 to 4 minutes. Add the flour and turmeric. Cook, stirring, for 1 minute. Add the milk, and bring to a boil, stirring constantly until thickened. Simmer for 5 minutes over a very low heat, stirring. Add the lemon juice and cilantro and season to taste.

❖ Steam the zucchini slices over boiling water for 5 minutes until just tender. Arrange them in the choux rings. Pour over the sauce and serve immediately.

BLACK BEAN TACOS
WITH ROASTED CORN CHILI SAUCE

SERVES 4 TO 8

TACOS ARE CRISP-FRIED TORTILLAS. YOU CAN BUY THEM
READY-MADE BUT IT'S BETTER TO FRY THE TORTILLAS
YOURSELF. TORTILLAS ARE TRADITIONALLY MADE WITH
MASA HARINA – DEHYDRATED MAIZE FLOUR. IT'S
DEFINITELY EASIER TO USE STORE-BOUGHT TORTILLAS.

2 tablespoons olive oil
1 onion, chopped finely
4 cloves garlic, chopped finely
4 fresh chilies, seeded and chopped
2 teaspoons ground cumin
1 tablespoon dried oregano
2⅔ cups cooked black kidney beans (1⅓ cups dry weight)

⅓ cup frozen corn kernels
1 x 14-ounce can chopped tomatoes
1¼ cups Vegetable Stock (page 111)
Salt and pepper
Peanut (or vegetable) oil for frying
8 tortillas

TO SERVE
Roasted Corn Chili Sauce (page 107)

❖ Heat the oil in a pan, and fry the onion and garlic gently over a low heat for 5 minutes until translucent. Add the chili, cumin and oregano, and stir-fry for a minute to release the flavor.

❖ Stir in the remaining ingredients, bring to a boil, and simmer over low heat for 20 minutes, stirring occasionally, until most of the liquid has evaporated.

❖ Shallow-fry the tortillas in very hot oil for 30 seconds until slightly browned. Drain on paper towels, and keep warm while you fry the rest.

❖ Form each tortilla into a boat shape in the palm of your hand, spoon in some of the filling, and top with the heated sauce. They will become crisp as you do so.

❖ Transfer to a warm serving dish into which all the tacos will just fit, and serve immediately.

CHILI AND CILANTRO CORN MUFFINS

MAKES 8

ROASTED GARLIC AND CHILI GIVE THESE QUICKLY MADE
MUFFINS A SPICY KICK. FOR THE BEST RESULTS, BAKE THEM
IN INDIVIDUAL HIGH-SIDED PIE TINS. OTHERWISE USE
REGULAR MUFFIN PANS.

2 large fresh green chilies
3 large cloves garlic, unpeeled
2 cups all-purpose flour
1 cup yellow cornmeal
1 tablespoon baking powder
3 eggs

5 tablespoons olive oil
5 tablespoons finely chopped cilantro
2 teaspoons brown sugar
1 teaspoon salt
¾ cup water

❖ Roast the chilies and garlic at 350°F for 15 minutes. Discard the skins and the chili seeds, and chop roughly. Place 8 oiled individual pie pans in the oven for 5 minutes.

❖ Sift the flour, cornmeal and baking powder together in a bowl.

❖ Put the chilies and garlic in a blender with the eggs, oil, cilantro, sugar and salt. Add the water, and process briefly until smooth. Add to the dry ingredients, whisking well to form a smooth batter.

❖ Divide the batter between the hot pans, and bake for 15 to 20 minutes.

SALSA VERDE (PIQUANT GREEN SAUCE)

MAKES ABOUT 1 GENEROUS CUP

3 shallots, chopped
9 tablespoons finely chopped parsley
6 tablespoons finely chopped basil
3 tablespoons capers, rinsed

2 cloves garlic, crushed
Grated zest of 1½ lemons
1½ tablespoons lemon juice
¾ cup olive oil
Salt and pepper

❖ Combine all the ingredients in a blender, and process until smooth. Check the seasoning, and add more salt and pepper if necessary. The sauce will keep in an airtight container in the refrigerator for a week. Bring to room temperature before serving.

ROASTED RED BELL PEPPER SAUCE

MAKES ABOUT 2 ½ CUPS

4 red bell peppers
2 tablespoons olive oil
1 onion, chopped finely
2 teaspoons finely chopped thyme
2 cloves garlic, chopped finely

4 tomatoes, peeled, seeded and chopped
1 tablespoon white wine vinegar
1¼ cups Vegetable Stock (page 111)
Salt and pepper
1 generous tablespoon butter

❖ Place the bell peppers under a hot broiler for about 15 minutes, turning frequently, until the skins begin to blister on all sides. Let cool, then remove the skins and seeds, and chop the flesh.
❖ Heat the oil in a saucepan, and fry the onion and thyme gently over low heat for 5 minutes until the onion is translucent. Add the garlic, and fry for another minute or two. Stir in the tomatoes, vinegar, stock, salt and pepper.
❖ Purée the mixture with the bell peppers by rubbing through a strainer. Return to the pan, bring to a boil and reduce slightly, then whisk in the butter.
❖ Check the seasoning, and serve either hot or at room temperature.

TANGY PEANUT SAUCE

MAKES ABOUT 1 CUP

¾ cup finely chopped peanuts
1 tablespoon wine vinegar
1 cup water

1 tablespoon tamari (Japanese soy sauce)

❖ Put all the ingredients in a food processor, and blend until smooth.
❖ Pour into a saucepan, and simmer over a medium-low heat, stirring, for 15 minutes, or until thickened.

CILANTRO SAUCE

MAKES ABOUT 1 ¼ CUPS

1½ cups cilantro, trimmed
½ cup flat-leafed Italian parsley, trimmed
2 scallions, chopped
1 clove garlic, crushed
2 tablespoons lime juice

1½ teaspoons toasted cumin seeds
¼ teaspoon salt
Pepper to taste
⅓ cup yogurt, strained through a cheesecloth
⅓ cup heavy cream

❖ Combine all the ingredients, except the yogurt and cream, in a food processor, and purée for 3 minutes, scraping the sides of the bowl frequently. Pour into a bowl, and stir in the yogurt and cream.

MINTED YOGURT SAUCE

MAKES ABOUT 1 ¼ CUPS

1¼ cups yogurt, strained through a cheescloth
1 clove garlic, crushed
1 teaspoons olive oil

½ teaspoon wine vinegar
Salt and pepper
4 tablespoons finely chopped mint

❖ Combine the ingredients in the order listed. Cover, and let stand for an hour before serving.

ROASTED CORN CHILI SAUCE

MAKES ABOUT 2 CUPS

2 ears corn with husks
2 fresh green chilies
2 tablespoons vegetable oil
½ onion, chopped
1 clove garlic, chopped finely

Scant 1¼ cups Vegetable Stock (page 111)
1¼ cups light cream
½ cup cilantro, stalks removed
2 tablespoons lime juice
Salt

❖ Roast the corn in their husks in the oven at 350°F for 10 minutes, turning occasionally. Add the chilies and roast for another 10 minutes.
❖ Let cool, then remove the husks, and cut the kernels from the cobs. Cut each cob stalk into three pieces. Peel the chilies, and remove the seeds.
❖ Heat the oil in a saucepan, and fry the cob stalks, onion and garlic gently over low heat for 3 to 4 minutes until the onion is translucent. Add the stock, raise the heat, and simmer for 10 minutes until the liquid is reduced slightly.
❖ Add the cream, and simmer for 10 minutes, stirring continuously as the liquid reduces.
❖ Remove the cob pieces with a slotted spoon, scraping off as much sauce as possible. Add two-thirds of the corn kernels, the chilies, cilantro and lime juice to the sauce. Liquidize in a blender until smooth. Stir in the remaining corn kernels. Season with salt to taste, reheat and serve.

TOMATO SAUCE

MAKES ABOUT 1 ⅔ CUPS

1 x 14-ounce can chopped tomatoes
Generous ¼ cup/½ stick butter
1 onion, halved
1 small strip lemon peel

1 clove garlic, chopped finely
2 teaspoons dried oregano
¼ teaspoon sugar
Salt and pepper

❖ Put all the ingredients in a saucepan. Simmer over a low heat for 45 minutes, uncovered, stirring occasionally. Discard the onion and lemon peel, and pour the mixture into a food processor. Blend until smooth, and then return to the pan. Check the seasoning, adding more salt, pepper or sugar as necessary.

SATAY SAUCE

MAKES ABOUT 2 CUPS

1 cup fresh peanuts, roasted
2 teaspoons coriander seeds, roasted
2 tablespoons vegetable oil
2 cloves garlic, chopped finely
1 shallot or ½ small onion, chopped finely
2 teaspoons finely chopped lemon grass (or ½ teaspoon dried)

½ teaspoon chili powder
1 teaspoon ground cumin seeds
2 cups water
1 teaspoon Indonesian soy sauce
1 teaspoon dark brown sugar
½ teaspoon salt
Juice of ½ lime or lemon
2 tablespoons plain yogurt
Freshly ground black pepper

❖ Put the peanuts and coriander seeds in a coffee grinder or blender, and grind as finely as possible.
❖ Heat the oil over a moderate heat in a saucepan. Add the garlic, shallot or small onion, lemon grass, chili powder and cumin seeds. Stir-fry for about 1 minute until lightly browned.
❖ Add the water, soy sauce, sugar, salt and peanut mixture. Bring to a boil, stirring. Reduce the heat, and simmer for 15 to 20 minutes until thickened, stirring frequently.
❖ Let cool slightly, then stir in the lime juice, yogurt and pepper.

SPICY GINGER AND SESAME SAUCE

MAKES ABOUT ⅔ CUP

2 teaspoons sesame seeds
½ cup peeled fresh ginger root, chopped finely
4 tablespoons rice vinegar (or wine vinegar)

7 teaspoons sugar
1 tablespoon tamari (Japanese soy sauce)
¼ teaspoon salt
1 teaspoon snipped chives

❖ Dry-fry the sesame seeds in a small heavy-based pan until they turn golden. Remove from the pan, and set aside.
❖ Put the ginger, vinegar, sugar, tamari and salt in a small bowl, and blend together until smooth and the sugar has dissolved.
❖ Pour into a small serving bowl, and stir in the sesame seeds and chives.
❖ Let stand at room temperature for at least 1 hour.

PEANUT SAUCE

MAKES ABOUT 1 ½ CUPS

1 tablespoon peanut oil
1 onion, chopped finely
½ green bell pepper, chopped finely
1 clove garlic, chopped finely
⅔ cup peeled and chopped tomatoes

½ cup finely chopped peanuts
½ teaspoon salt
Pepper
⅔ cup milk
2 teaspoons tamari (Japanese soy sauce)

❖ Heat the oil in a saucepan, and fry the onion and green bell pepper gently over low heat for 10 minutes. Add the garlic and tomatoes, and simmer for 10 minutes more, stirring occasionally.
❖ Liquidize in a blender with the nuts, salt and pepper.
❖ Return to the pan, add the milk, and simmer, uncovered for 10 minutes, stirring occasionally.
❖ Stir in the tamari just before serving.

CARROT AND CILANTRO RELISH

MAKES ABOUT ⅔ CUP

¾ cup grated carrot
2 tablespoons trimmed cilantro
2 tablespoons onion, chopped
1-inch piece fresh root ginger, chopped finely

1 green chili, seeded and chopped finely
2 tablespoons lemon juice
1 tablespoon sugar
½ teaspoon salt

❖ Combine all the ingredients in a food processor, and blend until smooth. Let stand at room temperature for at least 1 hour to let the flavors develop.

OLIVE AND CILANTRO RELISH

MAKES ABOUT ⅔ CUP

2 red bell peppers
1¼ cups black olives in oil, stoned and finely sliced
½ fresh green chili, seeded and chopped very finely
6 tablespoons finely chopped cilantro leaves

1 tablespoon lemon juice
pepper
5 tablespoons olive oil
Lettuce leaves
1 hard-cooked egg, quartered

❖ Place the bell peppers under a hot broiler for 10 minutes, turning occasionally, until the skins begin to blacken. Cover or place in a sealed plastic bag for 5 minutes. Remove the skin and seeds, and cut the flesh into small dice. Mix with the olives, chili and cilantro.
❖ Whisk together the lemon juice, pepper and olive oil, and pour over the olive mixture. Let stand for 1 hour.
❖ Pile the mixture on a bed of lettuce leaves, and top with the hard-cooked egg quarters.

CUCUMBER AND MANGO RAITA

MAKES ABOUT 1 ½ CUPS

½ cup peeled and finely chopped cucumber
½ teaspoon salt
1 large ripe mango
2 tablespoons lime juice

⅔ cup yogurt, strained through a cheesecloth
2 scallions, green part included, chopped finely
Pepper

❖ Sprinkle the cucumber with the salt, and let drain for 30 minutes.
❖ Chop the mango flesh, and mix with the drained cucumber and remaining ingredients.
❖ Let stand for 1 hour before serving.

PEAR AND WALNUT OIL DRESSING

MAKES ABOUT 6 TABLESPOONS

4 oz peeled and cored ripe pears, chopped roughly
1 tablespoon lemon juice
2 tablespoons walnut oil

2 tablespoons olive oil
1½ teaspoons green peppercorns
salt

❖ Put all the ingredients in a blender and process until smooth.

HAZELNUT AND ORANGE VINAIGRETTE

MAKES 6 TABLESPOONS

2 tablespoons orange juice
1 teaspoons white wine vinegar
Salt and pepper

¾-inch piece fresh ginger root
4 tablespoons hazelnut oil

❖ Combine the orange juice, vinegar, salt and pepper in a small bowl. Put the peeled ginger in a garlic press, and squeeze the juice into the dressing. Whisk in the oil.

PIZZA DOUGH

MAKES 2 X 12-INCH OR 4 X 8-INCH BASES

3¼ cups white bread flour
1½ teaspoons salt
¼-ounce envelope quick-rising active dry yeast

1 tablespoon extra virgin olive oil
1 cup tepid (105°F) water

❖ Sift the flour, salt and yeast into a bowl. Make a well in the center and pour in the oil and water. Stir vigorously, gradually drawing in the flour, to form a soft dough.
❖ Knead on a floured surface for at least 10 minutes until the dough feels silky smooth and springy.
❖ Place in an oiled bowl, turning the dough so it is covered with oil, and cover with plastic wrap. Let rise in a warm place for up to 2 hours until doubled in size.

VEGETABLE STOCK

MAKES ABOUT 2 QUARTS

2 tablespoons sunflower oil
3 onions, chopped
2 tablespoons each finely
chopped fresh parsley, tarragon,
basil and thyme
2 finely sliced zucchini
1 finely chopped fennel bulb
2 leeks, green parts included,
sliced finely

2 celery stalks, leaves included,
sliced finely
4 cloves garlic, peeled and left
whole
10 black peppercorns, coarsely
crushed
1 teaspoon salt

❖ Heat the oil in a large saucepan. Add the onions and herbs, and fry gently for 5 over low heat minutes, until the onion is translucent.
❖ Add the remaining ingredients, then cover and cook together over a low heat for 10 to 15 minutes, stirring occasionally.
❖ Add 2¼ quarts of water, bring to a boil, skim, and simmer, half-covered, for 30 minutes.
❖ Pour through a cheesecloth-lined strainer. The stock can be refrigerated for up to five days.

STRONG VEGETABLE STOCK

MAKES ABOUT 2 ¼ QUARTS

2 tablespoons sunflower oil
2 onions, chopped finely
2 leeks, green parts included,
sliced finely
3 carrots, sliced finely
3 celery stalks, sliced finely
1 celeriac, chopped
4 tomatoes, chopped
1 potato, chopped
½ small cabbage, chopped finely

1¼ cups finely chopped
mushrooms
6 cloves garlic, peeled and left
whole
2 bay leaves
1 cup roughly chopped parsley
3 sprigs thyme or marjoram
1 teaspoon salt
10 black peppercorns, coarsely
crushed

❖ Heat the oil in a large pan. Add all the ingredients and 1¼ cups water. Cover, and simmer over medium-low heat for 15 minutes. Add 2½ quarts water, bring to a boil, then simmer, half covered, for 1½ hours, stirring from time to time.
❖ Pour through a cheesecloth-lined strainer. Check the flavor, adding more seasoning if necessary. Reduce the stock further if you want a stronger flavor. It can be refrigerated for up to five days.

INDEX